AN UNCOMMON PASSAGE

AN UNCOMMON PASSAGE

Traveling through History on the Great Allegheny Passage Trail

EDWARD K. MULLER

PHOTOGRAPHS BY PAUL G WIEGMAN

University of Pittsburgh Press

A John D. S. and Aida C. Truxall Book

This publication is supported by a grant from
The Pittsburgh Foundation.

Text design and typesetting by Kachergis Book Design

Library of Congress Cataloging-in-Publication Data
An uncommon passage : traveling through history on the Great
Allegheny Passage Trail / [edited by] Edward K. Muller ; photographs
by Paul G. Wiegman.
      p. cm.
   Includes index.
   ISBN-13: 978-0-8229-4366-2 (cloth : alk. paper)
   ISBN-10: 0-8229-4366-2 (cloth : alk. paper)
   1. Great Allegheny Passage Region (Pa. and Md.)—History.
2. Natural history—Great Allegheny Passage Region (Pa. and Md.)
3. Great Allegheny Passage (Pa. and Md.)—History.   I. Muller,
Edward K.   II. Wiegman, Paul G.
   F157.A45U63 2009
   974.8′7—dc22
   2009029724

CONTENTS

Color photographs between chapters are by Paul g Wiegman.

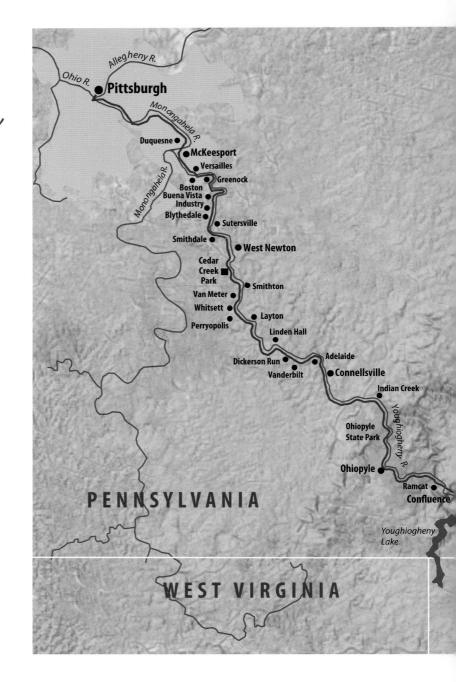

the Great Allegheny Passage Trail

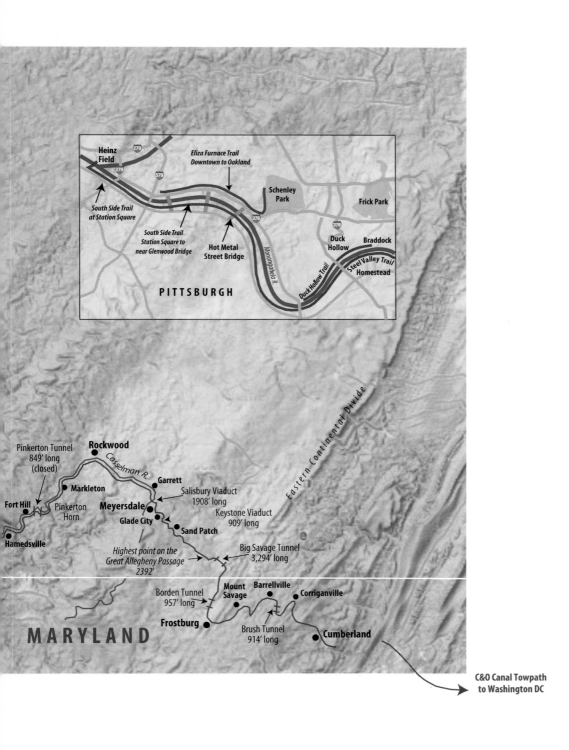

PITTSBURGH

Heinz Field

South Side Trail at Station Square

Eliza Furnace Trail Downtown to Oakland

Schenley Park

Frick Park

South Side Trail Station Square to near Glenwood Bridge

Hot Metal Street Bridge

Monongahela R.

Duck Hollow

Braddock

Duck Hollow Trail

Steel Valley Trail

Homestead

Eastern Continental Divide

Pinkerton Tunnel 849' long (closed)

Rockwood

Casselman R.

Garrett

Markleton

Salisbury Viaduct 1908' long

Fort Hill

Pinkerton Horn

Meyersdale

Keystone Viaduct 909' long

Glade City

Hamedsville

Sand Patch

Highest point on the Great Allegheny Passage 2392'

Big Savage Tunnel 3,294' long

Mount Savage

Barrellville

Corriganville

Borden Tunnel 957' long

Frostburg

Brush Tunnel 914' long

Cumberland

MARYLAND

C&O Canal Towpath to Washington DC

PREFACE

*W*hen my wife and I recently packed a lunch, loaded our bikes on the back of the car, and headed for a ride on the Great Allegheny Passage bike trail, we joined many others out to enjoy the year's waning warm weather and fall's colorful display. The trailhead parking lot overflowed with cars. People milled about in the visitors' center, bike shops, and restaurants. Couples, families, and more serious bikers distinguished by special clothing and faster speeds amicably shared the trail. Some cyclists turned off the trail and walked down to the river's edge; others rested on benches and logs where they could enjoy the forest's majesty. Periodically, a freight train pierced the sylvan scene as it rumbled through the valley on the other side of the river, a reminder that the trail runs along an abandoned railroad route.

This scene was replicated at many sites and trailheads along the Passage. It was exactly what a few visionaries pictured more than two decades ago when they requested funds from private foundations and public entities for building the bike trail. Imagine a trail, they challenged, running from Pittsburgh, Pennsylvania, through mountains and along river valleys of outstanding natural beauty and connecting with an existing trail at Cumberland, Maryland, to complete a route to Washington DC. A dream for these few, the trail seemed to many decision makers a low priority among numerous proposals purporting to address deindustrialization's devastating impact on southwestern Pennsylvania. Would a long-distance bike trail through the mountains generate the extensive use predicted by its most enthusiastic supporters, stimulate new businesses in small communities bypassed in the postindustrial age, and make the region more attractive to corporations seeking excellent places for their employees to live?

Today, the Great Allegheny Passage trail stretches for 150 miles from Pittsburgh to Cumberland, the culmination of years of hard work and fundraising by many people across the region. Accessing the trail at one of many possible points, most bikers undertake short day trips, returning to their cars after pedaling for a few hours. However, the number of bikers tackling the entire journey is rapidly increasing. The Passage follows railroad routes, which, along with early paths, trails, and roads, compose a corridor connecting the Mid-Atlantic region around the Potomac River Valley with the Ohio River Valley and the Midwest. Native Americans, British and colonial American soldiers, traders and settlers, teamsters, railroaders, and truckers all used the corridor to negotiate the Allegheny Mountains. Each phase of development altered and demolished much of the landscape of an earlier era such that travelers today see remnants of the many pasts, which can be appreciated through an understanding of the region's history.

The natural beauty and biking challenge of the Great Allegheny Passage trail are reasons enough to make the journey from Pittsburgh to Cumberland, and even beyond, to Washington DC. Knowing the historical significance of the Passage and its region, however, greatly enriches the experience. *An Uncommon Passage* introduces readers to the historical and geographical significance of the trail from a regional perspective. It is meant to complement guides that delineate mile by mile the specific phenomena that riders encounter.

Each contributor to this volume brings something unique to the understanding of the trail. Naturalist and photographer Paul g Wiegman describes the geology, rivers, and flora of the trail. While he paints with a broad brush in concert with the regional perspective of the book, he also identifies places to see examples of specific rock formations, woodland complexes, and wildflowers. Martin West, director of the Fort Ligonier Association, carefully recounts the struggle for control over the head of the Ohio River Valley between traditional European rivals France and Britain, in which the Great Allegheny Passage and Braddock's Road played such important roles. Historian Jennifer Ford picks up the story after the cessation of hostilities in 1763, tracing the course of settlement in the region into the early nineteenth century. Although farming and the typical frontier economy of scattered grist mills and whiskey distilleries, small market towns, and artisan shops emerged west of the Allegheny Mountains, early iron furnaces in the ridges of Maryland and Pennsylvania, as well as primitive harvesting of coal from abundant outcrops, foreshadowed the region's future. Former editor of *Carnegie Magazine* Robert Gangewere describes the transformation of the region's life and landscape by industrialization. Logging, coal mining, and coke manufacturing particularly scarred the landscape and, especially in the Connellsville coke district, darkened the sky. Cumberland became an industrial center, and Pittsburgh's legendary iron and steel industry spread up the banks of the Monongahela River, smoothing and extending the floodplain with fill, hardening river edges, and polluting the water. The railroads of the Passage spread throughout the region to facilitate this transformation.

Kevin Patrick, geographer at Indiana University of Pennsylvania, outlines the concerns of conservationists for industrialization's degradation of the natural landscape and sketches the subsequent development of environmental reforms and outdoor recreation over the past several decades. Abandoned rail lines provided the opportunity to reestablish the passage through the mountains for cycling and hiking travel, which, unlike that of the railroads or automobiles, resembles the slow pace and intimacy of eighteenth-century journeys. In the final chapter, Paul g Wiegman returns to recount the intriguing and remarkable process by which the bike trail moved from vision to reality.

In addition to the contributions of the authors of the various chapters, I gratefully received the invaluable assistance of several people in shepherding this book to publication. Well before anyone put pen to paper, Richard Malmstrom produced an inventory of photographic repositories in both western Maryland and southeastern Pennsylvania. Cynthia Miller, director of the University of Pittsburgh Press, took the lead in drawing together photographs for the volume, while Paul g Wiegman generously made available the extensive collection of photographs that he has taken over the years. Deborah Meade, managing editor, ironed out the kinks that inevitably emerge among essays written by several different authors. And Ann Walston, production director, ensured the result of this handsome book, pleasing to both the eye and touch.

AN UNCOMMON PASSAGE

AN UNCOMMON PASSAGE

An Introduction

EDWARD K. MULLER

To bike along the Great Allegheny Passage trail from Cumberland, Maryland, to Pittsburgh, Pennsylvania, is to journey through both time and space. The trail follows a historic route through the Allegheny Mountains, connecting the Potomac River watershed and the middle Atlantic coast to the Ohio River watershed and the nation's vast, midwestern interior. Native Americans, colonial armies, frontier trappers and traders, settlers, and railroads used this topographically dramatic and difficult corridor created by the valleys of Wills and Jennings creeks and of the Casselman, Youghiogheny, and Monongahela rivers. With careful observation and some informed imagination, today's biking enthusiasts can envision significant aspects of the nation's natural, military, settlement, economic, and environmental history, all while enjoying the beauty and challenge of a great biking adventure.

The Great Allegheny Passage bike trail is the culmination, indeed the triumph, of more than thirty years of vision and hard work by scores of volunteers and professionals of various skills and backgrounds. The plan in the early 1970s to abandon the Western Maryland Railway tracks between Cumberland, Maryland, and Connellsville, Pennsylvania, spurred first the railroad's managers and then the Western Pennsylvania Conservancy to envision a rail trail through the magnificent Allegheny Mountains. Over the following decade or so, negotiations, land purchases, and construction by the Conservancy and the Pennsylvania Department of Environmental Resources resulted in a completed eleven-mile trail between Confluence and Ohiopyle, Pennsylvania, in the late 1980s.

The closing of more railroad lines in the Pittsburgh region led to additional opportunities for creating rail trails. The abandonment of the Montour Railroad in 1984 initiated the construction of a trail running north and west around Pittsburgh from near McKeesport, Pennsylvania, at the junction of the Youghiogheny River with the Monongahela River, to the Ohio River near Coraopolis, a few miles northwest of the city. In the early 1990s, another group of volunteers formed the Regional Trail Corporation to build a trail along the recently abandoned Pittsburgh and Lake Erie (P&LE) railroad line between McKeesport and Connellsville.

The striking popularity of the initial segments of these trails encouraged others to turn former rail lines into biking trails and complete a trail from Pittsburgh through Connellsville and on to Cumberland, where it would link up with the extant, 184-mile Chesapeake and Ohio (C&O) Canal Towpath to Washington DC. Seven trail organizations in southwestern Pennsylvania and western Maryland, all working on specific segments of the grand vision, formed the Allegheny Trail Alliance (ATA) in 1995 as an umbrella organization to coordinate work, promote the entire project, and facilitate fundraising. With the help of local communities and county governments, private groups and businesses, and state and federal government agencies, the seven constituent trail organizations and the ATA have turned the dreams of the early advocates into reality. The seven trail organizations: Allegheny Highlands Trail Association in Maryland, Allegheny Highlands Trail of Maryland; Somerset County Rails to Trails Association, Allegheny Highlands Trail of Pennsylvania; Ohiopyle State Park, Youghiogheny River Trail South; Regional Trail Corporation, Youghiogheny River Trail North; Steel Heritage Corporation, Steel Valley Trail; Friends of the Riverfront, Three Rivers Heritage Trail; and Montour Trail Council, Montour Trail. The Allegheny Trail Alliance called the trail the Great Allegheny Passage, which was not a name used historically to identify the route or routes taken between the Potomac River and southwestern Pennsylvania. In order to avoid confusion, the name is adopted in this book to describe the various historic routes that are closely related to the trail and often included parts of it.

The word *passage* has several definitions. Among other things, it means a route, a progress of events, and a transition. The Great Allegheny Passage embraces all three of these. It has always been an important route linking two regions of the continent separated by rugged mountains. The Passage was an active part of historical events and, by connecting two disparate regions, it traced both natural and human transitions. Native Americans and Anglo-American colonial frontiersmen moved along the river valleys and through the water gaps to cross the mountain barrier separating the coastal and interior regions. Although the relatively more hospitable topography of the western third of the Passage encouraged permanent settlement by some of these early peoples, most of them saw the route as a means by which to conduct long-distance trade.

When the lands west of the Allegheny Mountains attracted Anglo-American interest, the Great Allegheny Passage proved instrumental in the progress of historical events. The Passage, in the form of a military road opened by Major General Edward Braddock in 1755, was an important, though not decisive, corridor in England's and the colonies' efforts to wrest control of the Ohio River Valley from the French and the Native Americans. As a result of England's 1763 victory in the French and Indian War, sometimes called the Seven Years' War or the War for Empire, Anglo-Americans settled these western lands instead of French *habitants* or later Canadians. Although Native Americans resisted colonization of the area for several more years after the French withdrew, making life on southwestern Pennsylvania's and western Maryland's frontier dangerous, they surrendered the territory to Anglo-American authority in 1768.

The Passage offered land-hungry Virginians access to the newly opening western country, where they soon came into conflict with settlers from eastern Pennsylvania filtering through the Allegheny Mountains by an alternative route. Pennsylvanians generally came west by Forbes Road, which, like Braddock's Road, followed former Native American paths and was hacked out of the wilderness by the military in the French and Indian War. Although the Virginians established the first effective Anglo-American settlement in the Youghiogheny and Monongahela river valleys, state authority and eventually cultural dominance was settled, after several years of struggle, in favor of Pennsylvania at the dawn of the new American nation. In 1780, the Mason-Dixon Line, initially surveyed in the 1760s to establish the boundary between Maryland and Pennsylvania, was extended westward to resolve the border dispute between Virginia and Pennsylvania.

Over the course of the nineteenth century, the Great Allegheny

Passage remained part of the American story. Now, instead of being central to a military drama, the Passage became a factor in the nation's rapid industrialization. Successful development depended on the ability to move agricultural products and natural resources such as timber, coal, and iron ore to Cumberland and Pittsburgh at the eastern and western ends, respectively, of the Passage. Opening in 1818, the National Road passed through Cumberland and ran a few miles west of the Passage. This new overland road temporarily diminished the Passage's significance as a route through the mountains. Seasonally dependent flatboats on the Potomac River, and later canal improvements between Cumberland and the coast, stimulated coal mining, lumbering, and iron making in western Maryland. Better navigation on the lower Youghiogheny and Monongahela rivers appealed to Pittsburgh merchants wanting to tap resources and expand trade in southwestern Pennsylvania. Private investors built primitive locks and dams to make the rivers more navigable. While the Youghiogheny system was a commercial failure, the locks and dams on the Monongahela enhanced the movement of agricultural products and coal from the Monongahela River Valley to Pittsburgh and downstream Ohio River Valley markets.

The coming of the railroads in mid-century ended the dreams of investors to improve the Youghiogheny River for commercial navigation and instead restored the importance of the Great Allegheny Passage. Pittsburgh was the prize for the eastern railroads. In the 1850s, Pittsburgh's ironmasters had initiated changes in the city's modest iron industry, which launched decades of explosive growth. By the end of the century, Pittsburgh's massive iron and steel industry had few rivals in America; the lower Monongahela River Valley had become known as the Steel Valley. The Pittsburgh area's many mills, numerous other industries, and residences consumed enormous quantities of southwestern Pennsylvania's coal resources, especially the superior coking coal of the Connellsville district.

Railroads running through the Youghiogheny River Valley connected many of these mines and coke works to the Pittsburgh market. The Pittsburgh and Connellsville Railroad began service to Connellsville in 1860, following the Youghiogheny's eastern bank. It was extended to Cumberland in 1871 with the support of the Baltimore and Ohio (B&O) Railroad, which had reached that Maryland city from Baltimore three decades earlier. The B&O took over the Pittsburgh and Connellsville a few years later. In the 1880s, the Pittsburgh, McKeesport, and Youghiogheny Railroad, constructed a line from Pittsburgh to Connellsville on the opposite bank of the river from the B&O; it was later absorbed into the P&LE. In 1912, the Western Maryland (WM) Railroad opened a route from Cumberland to Connellsville, where it connected with the P&LE. The WM took a different route from the B&O through the mountains between Cumberland and Meyersdale, Maryland, after which the two railroads closely paralleled each other to Pittsburgh, running on opposite river banks. Thus, two railroad routes ran along most of the Great Allegheny Passage, connecting Pittsburgh and Cumberland. They both transported the coal, timber, and quarry products of the region's rich natural resource industries and connected the vigorous urban industrial markets of the middle Atlantic and the Midwest.

While the mines, sawmills, quarries, and small factories arising with industrialization dominated the Great Allegheny Passage's life and landscape for more than one hundred years after the 1850s, the mountains and river valleys simultaneously attracted urban residents who enjoyed the beautiful scenery and outdoor recreation. The railroads provided the access. Even before the twentieth century began, resort hotels and camps drew customers from Pittsburgh, Baltimore, and Washington DC to the salubrious mountain environment. Hunting and fishing clubs as well as private cottages were located near railroad stops. However, the automobile, the Great Depression, and World War II curtailed this business, leaving older hotels tattered and forlorn or closed.

Even before the United States joined World War II, the market for the mountain region's natural resource products, especially coal, began to decline. After the war, coal mines and coke works closed, local manufacturers boarded up their small factories, unemployment spread, and many residents left to seek jobs in the Pittsburgh and Washington DC areas or elsewhere in the country. Even the mills of the Steel Valley, with the exception of the Edgar Thomson works in Braddock, fell silent in the 1980s and then were demolished in the 1990s. Freight trains and a few Amtrak passenger trains to Washington continued to move through the historic corridor between the East and Midwest, although eventually the Western Maryland and P&LE abandoned their lines. Only the B&O tracks, now part of the CSX system and still used by Amtrak, remain in use.

A combination of factors came together after 1950 to revive, indeed remarkably expand, recreational opportunities amidst the collapse of the traditional industrial economy. The nearly universal ownership of automobiles ended regional railroad passenger service, but the vastly improved highways actually enhanced access to the mountains. Flood-control projects for Pittsburgh created an impoundment reservoir or lake upstream from Confluence on the Youghiogheny River in 1948. Interest in water sports like whitewater rafting grew in both southwestern Pennsylvania and western Maryland, while conservationists, especially outdoor sportsmen's clubs and the Western

Pennsylvania Conservancy, worked to restore and preserve woodlands through the creation of state parks, forests, and game lands. By the 1960s, conservation had evolved into the environmental movement and fostered a burgeoning appreciation for the region's natural assets among a broader spectrum of the population than ever before.

Environmentalism expanded the conception of natural resources to include recreational opportunities, moving beyond the traditional view of them as simply for the production of raw materials and energy. Postwar prosperity, lasting until the 1970s for industrial workers, elevated many urbanites into a middle class with the leisure time, disposable income, and automobiles to take advantage of outdoor recreational activities from traditional hunting and fishing pursuits to more fashionable skiing, fly fishing, hiking, rock climbing, and kayaking ventures. Abandoned railroad tracks offered the ideal venue to add biking along a topographically friendly trail to the mix of activities, and in the process redefine the role of the Great Allegheny Passage in the postindustrial economy.

The Great Allegheny Passage has long revealed to those traveling along it important natural and cultural transitions. Journeying from Cumberland to Pittsburgh by foot or horse, early travelers intimately experienced three geological provinces—the Ridge and Valley Province of the Great Allegheny Passage's eastern end, the Allegheny Mountains of its middle section, and once over the Allegheny Front and continental divide the complexly eroded Allegheny Plateau of the western end. They passed through a water gap, the Narrows, in breeching the brief Ridge and Valley section in Maryland before tackling the mountains. In the mountains, deep gorges carved by running waters and man-made cuts made later exposed rock formations that revealed the story of millions of years of massive geological forces and change. Leaving behind the water gap of the final western ridge, Chestnut Ridge, travelers encountered a less formidable area of slower, meandering rivers and shallower, wooded valleys. Observant wayfarers also noticed changes in forest composition roughly approximating the transition in altitude and geological provinces. Their journey passed through the northern extent of the southern forest complex, which at higher altitudes yielded to the southern extent of northern forests. In turn, different woodland compositions prevailed in the valleys or "coves" of the western ridges and the valleys of the Allegheny Plateau.

Human transitions along the passage have been no less profound than the natural ones. In the mid-eighteenth century, travelers moved from the settled east to the frontier west, from a world of Anglo-American settlement to that of Native Americans and a thin veneer of French military presence. After Pennsylvania took control of the western half of the passage in 1780, travelers journeying from the Potomac River to the lower Youghiogheny River left the South and entered the North, moving between two distinctive American cultural regions. In crossing the Mason-Dixon Line, they experienced contrasts in the spoken language, house styles, food preferences, and, until the 1860s, the fact of slavery.

As the nineteenth century wore on, the transitions between rural and urban landscapes became more palpable. After traversing the industrial landscape of Cumberland and Frostburg, the natural grandeur of the mountains and rivers, occasional farms, visible evidence of logging and mining, and small market towns dominated vistas for approximately seventy-five miles. When travelers descended to the Allegheny Plateau at Connellsville, industry and mining replaced the serenity of the rural landscape. Coal tipples, gob piles, the smoke and din of coke works, and company towns signaled the change. Just as the rushing waters of the lower Youghiogheny flowed toward their absorption into the big, muddy, and polluted Monongahela River crowded with enormous coal tows, travelers approaching the river's junction at McKeesport sensed the awesome presence of America's archetypal industrial city—the smoky city of Pittsburgh. The contrast of the final fifteen miles to Pittsburgh, through Andrew Carnegie's empire (after 1901 U.S. Steel's) and past the gigantic Jones and Laughlin (J&L) iron and steel works, could not have differed more profoundly with the Passage's earlier years and its enduring natural beauty in the mountains and river gorges. Although the industrial landscape has largely disappeared, today's bikers still experience the rural-urban dichotomy.

The hard edges of an urban landscape account for roughly 15 percent of the 150-mile-long Great Allegheny Passage. Once the eastward-bound rider reaches the small community of Boston, four miles south of McKeesport and about twenty miles from Pittsburgh, only Connellsville interrupts the journey with a significant stretch of urban life until the trail descends into Frostburg and, fifteen miles later, into Cumberland. Despite the highly rural and often wilderness character of much of the trail, the astute traveler understands that in its role as route, the Passage pulled these distant lands into the metropolitan orbit of Baltimore, Washington DC, and Pittsburgh, knitting them all into whole cloth. American cities have functioned in a close, though not necessarily harmonious, relationship with their surrounding hinterlands. Merchants from Georgetown (until 1871, then Washington DC) and Baltimore coveted the timber and coal of western Maryland, and advocated the improvement of transportation in order to access those resources. Metropolitan capital flowed into the region to develop the mines, factories, and logging operations that transformed the landscape. After 1920, when resource exploitation and manufacturing slowed, many residents left the region to find work and start new lives in the rapidly growing Baltimore-Washington metropolitan complex.

Pittsburgh had a similar metropolitan relationship with the western portion of the Passage. From its beginning in the late eighteenth century, Pittsburgh depended on the surrounding countryside for food and fuel while, in turn, rural residents and businesses often looked to that city's merchants for consumer goods and capital. In the early years of difficult overland travel, the farms and hamlets of the Youghiogheny and Monongahela valleys were remote from the city in the sense of direct contact. Most rural residents likely never set foot in Pittsburgh, yet the city's markets and its political and financial influence were nonetheless real factors in southwestern Pennsylvania's life. Thus, in the violent Whiskey Rebellion of 1794, which erupted in the region over the federal government's imposition of a tax on distilled spirits, the enraged rebels of the countryside mustered at Braddock's Fields several miles south of Pittsburgh where Turtle Creek meets the Monongahela and threatened to march on Pittsburgh as the locus and symbol of merchant power and federal authority. Only cooler heads defused the situation, but the intimate and complex relationship of city and region was clearly demonstrated.

With rapid growth and industrialization, Pittsburgh and its many surrounding mill towns expanded their dependence on the Youghiogheny Valley and the Allegheny Mountains for enormous quantities of building supplies and fuel, especially coal and coke. City financiers and industrialists helped to develop these resources. The flow of capital through loans, partnerships, corporate mergers and takeovers, and branch plants, along with the extensive railroad network, industrialized the countryside and drew it into an even tighter web of economic relationships with the city.

The generally well-known business career of Henry Clay Frick illustrates the kinds of links that tied the metropolis and region together. As a young man of twenty in 1869, Frick worked as a bookkeeper for his grandfather, Abraham Overholt, in Broad Ford, Pennsylvania, a site northwest of Connellsville on the Youghiogheny, now part of the trail. Overholt operated two rye whiskey distilleries, a flour mill, a timber business, and a farm. Although born and raised in the shadow of Chestnut Ridge, Frick had already worked and lived briefly in Pittsburgh before returning to his family's extensive rural industries in Fayette and Westmoreland counties. In 1871, he began investing in coal resources and the manufacture of coke for the voracious appetite of Pittsburgh's iron and steel industry. With the financial backing of Pittsburgh financiers, notably but not exclusively that of Judge Thomas Mellon and his sons, he built a formidable position in the Connellsville coke industry by 1880. In that year, Frick moved his residence to Pittsburgh and ran his coke firm by telegraphic communication, the use of frequent commuter railroad service from the city, and, of course, the supervision of managers in the field. The relationship between H. C. Frick Coke Company and Pittsburgh grew even closer when Andrew Carnegie purchased half of the firm for his iron and steel companies and expanded his stake over the next several years. With this corporate association and its deep pockets, Frick built his company into the industry's dominant force in the coke region. In 1889, Carnegie selected Frick to run his steel complex. From his Pittsburgh office, Frick's decisions about corporate investments, business operations, and labor relations affected life throughout the Youghiogheny and Monongahela valleys.

Although the methodical, uncompromising, and at times imperious Frick, standing at the helm of Carnegie's steel empire, may have been the most visible presence of Pittsburgh's reach into the Pennsylvania portion of the Great Allegheny Passage region, many other of the city's corporations, mining firms, and investment houses operated there as well. By 1920, steel works had crept along the Monongahela River to sites less than ten miles from the traditional coke district. Big firms like U.S. Steel and J&L operated their own captive mines and coke plants. In western Maryland, Consolidated Coal Corporation seemed even more omnipotent.

Electronic communication in the twentieth century also tied the rural communities to their respective metropolitan markets. Although newspapers and catalog sales had always diminished the distance between city and country, first the radio in the 1920s and later television in the 1950s reached residents throughout the regional hinterlands. Through these media, metropolitan life—its news, fashion, sports, music, and other forms of entertainment—gained an unprecedented immediacy for rural residents.

The relationship between metropolis and region took on an additional dimension when city residents sought the recreational opportunities of the Allegheny Mountains. Instead of exhausting their natural resources to feed the city's industrial appetite, and sending their young men and women to work in the metropolis, regional residents discovered that they also had a renewable resource to offer urbanites. Pittsburghers not only rode the trains and later drove their cars to enjoy the mountains, but some also built second homes and eventually retired in the area. In turn, local entrepreneurs advertised the attractions of the Laurel Highlands, as the area has been named for marketing purposes, in Pittsburgh and the Baltimore-Washington metropolitan areas. Whereas the cities had always reached out to penetrate and develop the countryside of western Maryland and southwestern Pennsylvania for their own goals, these areas now are reaching back to the urban centers for their own ends. The Great Allegheny Passage bike trail and its Potomac partner, the C&O Canal Towpath, literally strengthen the relationship between the great metropolitan cities at the eastern and western termini and their hinterlands.

More than a bike trail of exceptional beauty and recreational adventure, the Great Allegheny Passage offers a route into our nation's and region's history. Cyclists explore through the remnant landscapes and in their historical imagination a path central to the nation's colonial struggles of imperial rivalry, its pioneer settlement and massive industrialization, its feats of transportation technology, and its economic and social transformation at the end of the twentieth century. The Great Allegheny Passage itself is a part of that transformation. *An Uncommon Passage* is a guide to that history and geography.

Cyclists on the Eliza Furnace Trail in Pittsburgh.

(left) Riverton Bridge across the Monongahela River at McKeesport.

Remains of Banning Mine #4, near West Newton.

(left) Original Pittsburgh & Lake Erie tracks at crossing near Sutersville.

Between Hays and Pittsburgh.

Cyclists along the trail just south of Industry, between McKeesport and Connellsville.

THE LIVING PASSAGE

Flora, Fauna, and the Natural Environment

PAUL G WIEGMAN

*I*n all the effortless grandeur that is evident in the forests, wildflowers, wild rivers, and scenic views along the Great Allegheny Passage, you as the visitor will need to stop occasionally and listen to the ancient story that the rocks have to tell.

The foundation geology of the region through which the Great Allegheny Passage passes provides the setting. The water sculpted the raw stone, and the rivers cut the path for the trail to follow. Water and gravity collectively carved a sometimes gentle, sometimes abrupt corridor through mountains and deep into plateaus, a course that would be followed first by Native Americans on foot, then explorers on foot and with wagons and artillery, then humans seeking the easiest path for their bulky steam locomotives to negotiate. Thank the rivers for the easy ride through the mountains and think about the effort it would take to go over them if the water had not carved deep gaps. You will have plenty of opportunity since the waters, still and silent or tumbling and raucous, are never far away.

Youghiogheny River Water Gap between Confluence and Ohiopyle from an overlook at the summit of Laurel Ridge on the Laurel Highlands hiking trail. Photograph by Paul g Wiegman.

The length of the Great Allegheny Passage takes a traveler through more than 400 million years of time. The rock outcrops and layers that solemnly stand guard along the side of the trail have seen most of the history of terrestrial life on earth—from the first creatures to crawl out of primordial seas, to giant tree ferns and enormous land lizards, to the birth of flowering plants, and finally to the arrival of humans.

The Great Allegheny Passage provides an exceptional and intimate view of the intricate geology of the region from Cumberland, Maryland, to Pittsburgh, Pennsylvania. The fundamental pattern along the trail is layered rocks of sedimentary origin. They are pages of a book written half a billion years ago. Since "published," the text has been pushed, pulled, and otherwise shaped by continental forces. The landscape we see now is a result of geologically recent processes of uplift of the land from sea level to present elevations, and then the inexorable erosion by wind and water.

Lush forests once blanketed the landscape of the Ridge and Valley Province around Cumberland, and spread thickly across the Allegheny Mountains to, and including, the Pittsburgh Plateau Province surrounding Pittsburgh. Now, forests, farm fields, and human habitations spread over the land, but just as the primeval forests did, they hide the primal rock layers.

Still, there are numerous places where natural and human excavations have exposed the base rock along the Great Allegheny Passage so that the origin of the terrain can be determined. Scattered along the winding path are edgewise glimpses of ancient rock layers that, when read correctly, tell the story of events that took place so long ago.

Stopping alongside a towering rock face of sandstone and running a hand over delicate, finely textured patterns that were swirled from shifting sand eons ago, it is difficult to grasp the scale of time the cold surface has survived. We think in lifetimes that span less than a century; forests surrounding the rock face multiply that period several times. The age of the rock, mountains, rivers, and, ultimately, the whole of the landscape itself, is difficult to grasp.

These cross-section views into the geologic past are the result of the tireless energy of water that begins as rain; then becomes groundwater and seeps; then forms rivulets, runs, creeks, streams, and finally rivers. All the time powered by gravity, water has unceasingly eroded the terrain. It has carved narrow gullies, sinuous valleys, deep gorges, and vast water gaps. The Great Allegheny Passage follows the major rivers of the region and finds the best and most abundant places that offer glimpses into the hearts of mountains and the geologic stories that would otherwise be hidden.

The gradual gradient necessary for the railroads to cross the Allegheny Front required builders to cut notches in steep valley slopes and shortcuts through fingers of mountain irregularities. The flow of the rails, as they followed the flow of the rivers, exposed even more chapters of the foundation geology.

For the visitor, the Great Allegheny Passage experience can involve reading a chronology that goes back millions of years. The narrative begins with mountains the immensity of the Rockies that loomed in what would much later become eastern Pennsylvania. Detritus of the inevitable erosion was the raw material for layered rocks along the trail today. Over time, sandy beaches cemented and compressed to become sandstone. Mudflats became slate. Where organic litter accumulated from coral reefs and teeming swarms of shelled creatures that basked in warm waters, limestone formed. Dark, murky, endless tree fern swamps became black veins of coal. Remains of the past built the flat alternating layers that are the foundation of this region.

The rock along the trail was at one time much like a ream of paper. The shifting of the continents led North America to collide with Africa. The colossal pressure of the impact slowly folded what seems to us to be rigid stone. From the collision, the Ridge and Valley Province of central Pennsylvania was given its basic shape with undulating, narrow ridges separated by confined valleys.

After that continental collision 200 million years ago, the plates drifted apart and erosion leveled the mountains to sea level. Continental pressures re-exerted themselves and uplift elevated the flat coastal surface. Rivers partnered with gravity and, rejuvenated, they began eroding the landscape once more. Over eons, the roots of the old, folded mountains were exposed, revealing the long, narrow ridges again. Haystack and Wills mountains, prominent features at the eastern end of the Great Allegheny Passage, were unmasked.

Not much of the Great Allegheny Passage is located in the Ridge

Layered rock strata along the Great Allegheny Passage in Ohiopyle State Park. Photograph by Paul g Wiegman.

and Valley Province. After cutting through the Narrows, a spectacular passage west of Cumberland, and following the line of Wills Mountain for a short span, it turns west and starts the long climb up the eastern slope of Big Savage Mountain. Along this stretch, the trail is on some of the oldest rocks in the region. Rock layers in the Wills Creek Valley were laid down 360 to 408 million years ago in a time called the Devonian age.

Turning west from Wills Creek and climbing the Allegheny Front, the trail passes through younger—if 40 million fewer years can be considered younger—rock layers from the Mississippian age. These were fashioned a mere 320 to 360 million years ago. Finally, near the summit of Big Savage Mountain, the relatively new rocks—only 286 to 320 million years old—are from the Pennsylvanian age. Once over the Big Savage, the trail mostly remains on this youthful foundation.

The Big Savage Mountain, a part of the larger Allegheny Front is the transition into a new geologic province, the Ridge and Valley Province is behind and the Allegheny Plateau—that extends from upstate New York to Alabama—is ahead. It is the largest landform province in the Appalachian Mountains.

The ascent up the Allegheny Front leads to another major landmark—the Eastern Continental Divide. Just east of the Big Savage Mountain Tunnel is a low ridge that parts the rainfall and sends it either east to the Potomac Basin, the Chesapeake Bay, and, finally, the Atlantic, or west, where water glides into various streams and rivers that ultimately lead to the Ohio River, the Mississippi, and the Gulf of Mexico.

The base rock of the Allegheny Plateau experienced the same sedimentary and erosion events that formed the layers of the Ridge and Valley Province. Yet the plateau area remained largely undistorted, folding only at the Allegheny Mountains. These mountains are folded, horizontal layers of various types of rock that were once great peaks. Over time, they were eroded to sea level and flattened, but below the tabletop-like surface, tortured mountain roots remained.

Across the plain covering the Alleghenies an ancient, north-flowing river, today called the Youghiogheny, meandered lazily without the driving power of gravity. Again, continental movements created pressure

Vista of the Ridge and Valley Province from just outside the southeast portal of the Big Savage Tunnel. Photograph by Paul g Wiegman.

and the land slowly rose. The higher the land ascended, the greater the power of the river became and the further it gouged into the surface of the rock. Soft sedimentary rocks were easily eroded and washed away. When the streams finally reached the hardest layers, erosion slowed. The corrugated shape of the original Allegheny Mountains, still present in the folded roots, was again exposed. The rock pleats of Chestnut and Laurel ridges, Negro Mountain, and Big Savage Mountain reappeared, echoing the Alleghenies of the past.

As the land rose, many streams conformed to the new topography, but the ancestral Youghiogheny was strong and the old folds were no match for the river. Churning waters, containing gritty sands suspended in the flow that gave it even more muscle, cut through the hardest of rock and carved deep gorges through Laurel and Chestnut ridges. Much of Ohiopyle State Park protects these magnificent landforms, which geologists call water gaps—places where rivers cross folded mountains at nearly right angles.

The deepest of the water gaps is through Laurel Ridge. Just five miles after first meeting the Youghiogheny River, the Great Allegheny Passage penetrates the heart of Laurel Ridge. The summits to the northeast and southwest reach over 2,900 feet above sea level. Eroding faster than the land rose, the river carved a gap 1,700 feet deep. Similar water gaps, but shallower, were formed through Chestnut Ridge and where Wills Creek cut through Haystack and Wills mountains and formed the Narrows.

The exposed rock layers from the pinnacle of Big Savage Mountain to the exit of Chestnut Ridge water gap are geologically described as the Pottsville series. This layer was formed during the Pennsylvanian age, when the land we bike on today was near the equator and was made up of shallow, tropical seas and lush, steamy wetlands. The

Ohiopyle Falls on the Youghiogheny River. Photograph by Paul g Wiegman.

massive, gray sandstone of the Pottsville series is particularly dense, hard, and resistant to erosion. The most easily seen portion appears at the ledges in Ohiopyle State Park where the Youghiogheny River cascades for several hundred feet over numerous small steps before finally falling twenty feet over Ohiopyle Falls.

The Pottsville series indirectly defines the biota of the region. Rare plants are harbored in the scoured rock river edges in and around Ohiopyle. Allegheny wood rats make their homes in tumbled rock scree on the slopes. Once abundant over a large range, the Allegheny wood rat is a small, sleek, light gray—a shade that matches the sandstone—woodland animal with a bushy tail. The rats live where blocks of rock are just beginning to separate from the buried layer, and have formed labyrinths, vertical cliffs, and smaller bits of stone in rubble fields. The wood rats build nests deep in this maze of small passages. Recently, the Allegheny wood rat population has declined for unknown reasons. One may be the loss of suitable mature forest habitat with sufficient oaks to provide a constant food supply of acorns. The Allegheny wood rat is now on the Endangered Species List for Pennsylvania.

Another rare species of the sandstone blocks is the green salamander. This small, solitary amphibian reaches the northern limit of its range on the south side of the Chestnut Ridge water gap. Apparently the Youghiogheny River is a formidable barrier to the further northern dispersal of the tiny and fragile salamander. Green salamanders are secretive and difficult to see. They live in deep, horizontal crevices of sandstone blocks where temperature and moisture is constant. They may venture outside of their broad, low-ceilinged homes on late summer evenings during a light rain, a time when most humans are huddled in their own homes.

The plants are also influenced by the Pottsville series. Rhododendrons thrive in the acid soils of the sandstone. A glimpse of the vegetation from the time when this rock was formed is evident quite near to the Great Allegheny Passage, on the river ledges just downstream of the low bridge at Ohiopyle. A trail leading from the staircase off the west side of the bridge, beyond the restored rail station, follows the river. A few hundred feet after the bridge is the fossil imprint of a tree fern. The odd, concave indention with the surface of the ancient plant still prominent illustrates the tropical origins of the rock and the vegetation that once grew in this place.

Ohiopyle is not the only place where the dense, gray Pottsville sandstone makes an appearance; it is ubiquitous along the Passage from Meyersdale to Connellsville, especially in the rapids of the Casselman and Youghiogheny rivers and in places where narrow cuts with jagged walls line the trail. Because of the undulating folds of the Allegheny ridges, the sandstone layer is both the rock creating the rapids and falls at the bottom of the valley, and the rock of the vertical cliffs and overlooks at the summit of the ridges. On the road between Ohiopyle and Confluence, the spectacular overlook called Bachman Rocks offers grand views of the Laurel Ridge water gap and is another showcase for Pottsville sandstone.

Kayaker on the Youghiogheny River. Photograph by Paul g Wiegman.

Rafters on the Youghiogheny are acutely aware of the Pottsville series. Along the river from Confluence to Ohiopyle and then on to Burner Run, the intrepid floaters in rubber bubbles dodge all sizes of cobble and boulders of the great, gray sandstone. These river obstacles have been washed into the main stem from tributary streams such as Meadow, Cucumber, Bear, Bruner, Sheepskin, and Laurel runs. The Pottsville sandstone is the rock that churns the Youghiogheny milk-white and crafts the complicated rapids for which the river is famous.

Beyond the mountains, ridges, and water gaps, the Great Allegheny Passage passes into another, distinctly different, portion of the Allegheny Plateau—the Pittsburgh Plateau Province. If you have been riding along the Passage and have grown accustomed to rising cliffs beside the path, now, as the trail approaches Connellsville, you will feel as if you are coming out a tunnel without a roof. The steep walls of Chestnut Ridge disappear. There is no longer a view of the terrain ahead. Instead, the industrial, urban, and residential views of Connellsville signal that the land is different. It is flatter and more appropriate to human settlement. For the moment, natural wildness is behind you.

Geologically, the area that the trail traverses from here to its

Youghiogheny River at Cedar Creek near West Newton. Photograph by Paul g Wiegman.

western end is formed over sedimentary rocks that are the same age as those that stood beside you from the Allegheny Mountain to this point. Unlike the Alleghenies, however, the layers west of Connellsville are unfolded—a pile of pancake-flat slabs. This is the heart of the Allegheny Plateau Province and is well exemplified by the Pittsburgh Plateau. It is difficult to see the character of the section from the Great Allegheny Passage because from valley bottoms, the uniformity of the plateau's elevation is not readily apparent. To see the old plain, you need to get on top of a high point and scan the horizon. When you do, you see a skyline that is flat. This is the original surface of the terrain prior to uplift. This suggests that many of the place names of the uplands, such as Rich Hill, Kilndigging Hill, and Mount Vernon, are misnomers. The region is a flatland, a terrain that was once a low, uniform elevation. When you are on the plateau, you are never going up or down a hill—you are going into, or out of, a valley.

The layer-cake geologic foundation of this region is best seen along the trail near the I-70 bridge over the Youghiogheny. West of the trail are cliffs layered with various types of sedimentary rock. Even to the non-geologist, it is evident that the different layers are of dissimilar composition. Sandstone, slate, coal, and limestone are displayed for several miles.

In the Alleghenies, the major streams flow in confined valleys between summits and are fed by smaller perpendicular streams tumbling off the slopes. In the Pittsburgh Plateau, streams are treelike—geologists use the term Dendritic. The major waterways are the trunks, and the smaller creeks and runs are branches coming in at random angles and places, the rivulets are the twigs. Here, the long narrow ridges do not dictate drainages that look, from the air, like trellises. The Great Allegheny Passage in the Pittsburgh Plateau is crossed in many places by these tributaries. The high elevations on rounded knobs in the region reach peaks around 1,300 feet, and most of the streams occur around the base of Chestnut Ridge, where the folded area begins. Steep, narrow valleys contain and guide waterways with names like Furnace, Wildcat, and Virgin runs that sparkle and sing in the spring, whisper through the summer, and are silent and nearly dry in fall.

At McKeesport, the Youghiogheny ends in a confluence with the equally ancient Monongahela River. The Mon, as it is nicknamed in western Pennsylvania, is a river that has seen the region change over eons. At one time, the river slowly, lazily meandered over a landscape

Eli's Glen in Ohiopyle State Park. Photograph by Paul g Wiegman.

worn down to sea level. Uplift gave new energy to the water, and it began again to cut into the foundation rock. The red-tailed hawk sees the Monongahela from a view that demonstrates how the great bends of the old meanders are now cut deeply into the risen plateau. The river snakes north in gigantic curves and loops to its meeting with the Allegheny River at Pittsburgh's "Point."

Amid the ancient foundations of the Great Allegheny Passage, the traveler encounters an incongruity. Near Port Royal is some of the youngest rock on the planet—tufa. Found a quarter-mile south of Cedar Creek Park, these fragile limestone mounds are merely thousands of years old, and a thin layer on the surface may be only days or hours old. They are examples of new rock being formed from old, as carbonate materials are dissolved from foundation layers by groundwater. Once the water reaches the surface, the calcium comes out of solution and new rock is formed. The mounds, covered with moss, are similar in origin to stalactites and stalagmites found in caves.

All along the Great Allegheny Passage, rivers are a dominant part of the experience, and big waters are a collection of smaller waters. As the trail winds along the corridor, other tributary streams, each with a distinctive cascading voice, join in harmony with the Casselman, the Youghiogheny, and the Monongahela rivers. Streams with wild-sounding names like Stoney Batter Run, Wildcat Run, Ramcat Run, Bear Run,

Tufa formation at Port Royal, south of Cedar Creek Park in Westmoreland County. Photograph by Paul g Wiegman.

35

Crooked Run, Cedar Creek, and Deadman's Hollow are part of the greater experience. Each flow adds its own increment to the growing central river and, with every additional cubic foot of water, the power of the river grows.

Just west of Cumberland, at Kreigbaum, the former Western Maryland and the B&O railroads part company on the west side of the Narrows through Wills and Haystack mountains. The B&O follows Wills Creek, and the Western Maryland, and thus now the Great Allegheny Passage, head for Frostburg on a more circuitous route along Jennings Creek, a tributary of Wills Creek.

Past the town of Barrelville and on to Mount Savage, the trail clings to slopes above Jennings Creek. Climbing past the town of Zihlman, the route finally leaves the confines of the stream's watershed and wanders across the high headwaters of smaller streams with names known only to those living beside them. Finally, it skirts the base of Big Savage Mountain, waiting for the just the right opportunity to breach the barrier and break across the great divide that separates the waters on a continent. It's looking for an entrance to the Mississippi Basin.

At 2,400 feet elevation, on the east flank of the Big Savage Mountain, the Great Allegheny Passage plunges into the heart of the mountain, then emerges three-quarters of a mile later and stretches across the headwaters of Laurel Run. There the trail goes under McKenzie Hollow Road and enters the headwaters of the Flaugherty Creek, a gentle stream. The Great Allegheny Passage follows the water and, at the town of Sand Patch, rejoins the B&O right-of-way for a tandem run all the way to the Monongahela, one hundred miles to the west. At Meyersdale, Flaugherty gives its mountain waters to the Casselman, the first of several river exchanges that will take place before the water passes the Point at Pittsburgh.

Cyclists crossing the Salisbury Viaduct. Photograph by Paul g Wiegman.

The Casselman is born in the mountains of western Maryland. It begins in the Glades and Cunningham Swamp, wetlands on the west flank of Meadow Mountain—the name given to the continental divide in Maryland. By the time the Casselman gets to Meyersdale, it is a full-grown river.

One of the highlights of the Great Allegheny Passage is crossing the Salisbury Viaduct, a long, arrow-straight structure that spans the broad river valley that also contains old Route 219, new Route 219, and the river itself. The high vantage provides a grand view of the Casselman. Seen from both sides of the viaduct, the river lazily flows between fertile fields. At this point there is not a hint of the turmoil that the waters will engender further along their journey.

From the Salisbury Viaduct, a different kind of river can be seen. Towering against the western skyline, eight wind turbines rise from a former strip mine. The giant, triple blades slowly spin in the steady wind. The machines are drawing energy from a river of air flowing up and over the Allegheny Mountains, which passes over western Pennsylvania and is then squeezed between rising land below and different, immovable air currents above. Flowing into a narrower space above the land surface, the winds speed up and the turbines stand ready to capture the clean energy.

Near the town of Garrett, the quiet Casselman begins to find its voice. Next to the Great Allegheny Passage parking area south of Garrett, Bigby Creek is the first big tributary the trail crosses. In spring, the stream is a noisy torrent—a sound that is echoed by the Casselman and for many miles along the remainder of the trail. Beyond the parking area, the Passage follows a small road that hugs the river. Just downstream, the channel narrows and the river whitens and begins to sing—softly at first, as patches of foam break the smooth, green-gray surface. From here, the trail and the river enter an area bereft of human contrivances and dominated by wildness.

West of Garrett, the river valley narrows and steepens. The twin paths of river and trail cut through the northeastern edge of Negro Mountain. Lick Run appears about a third of the way to Rockwood, a Pennsylvania trail town, and is a prominent tributary that plunges over nine hundred feet in just over two and a half miles to catch the Casselman.

From a distance, the Casselman is like most other rivers. The sometimes still, sometimes swift, sometimes churning waters look inviting filled with life. The view from far off, however, is deceiving. Before human settlement, the river teemed with life—big fish, little fish,

Spring foliage near Lick Run in the Negro Mountain Water Gap northwest of Garrett. Photograph by Paul g Wiegman.

insects on the surface, insect larvae clinging to rocks, and all manner of aquatic creatures swimming, crawling, living, mating, and generally thriving in clean mountain water. Now, and hopefully just for the moment, that is not the case. A variety of insults on the crystal waters have left them sterile, virtually devoid of life. Industrial wastes, human wastes, and the final assassin, acid water from abandoned coal mines, were dumped into the Casselman without thought of the consequences. The breaking point was reached, and life abandoned the river.

More recently, efforts have focused on controlling wastes discharged into the waters, but the acid mine drainage has proven to be a greater challenge. Enormous underground reservoirs of water that had seeped into abandoned mines have accumulated. Mine entrances were plugged to confine the sulfur-rich water, but the pressure of the mine lakes overwhelmed efforts to contain them, the plugs failed, and ruptures dumped millions of gallons of acid water into the Casselman. The death toll is often described in the number of fish because they are the most easily seen corpses. The cost in smaller creatures and plants is staggering, and unfortunately never a part of the body count. Efforts continue to control and treat the legacy of the mines. The river is slowly regaining its health. If treatment continues and succeeds, future generations will enjoy a Casselman that once again brims with the multitude of creatures it once cradled.

Tributaries encountered along the trail are not the only waters that build rivers. In the area around Rockwood, in particular, and other places throughout the corridor, rivulets that sing only in spring have not yet had the time to carve valleys of their own, and simply plunge willy-nilly down rock cliffs. Thin streams of silver-white water roll from wooded slopes onto sheer rock walls that edge the Passage. Eventually, these waters find passage to the river.

In many other places, water has not even had the time to coalesce into rivulets. Sheer, smooth, stone walls glisten with a silent, slow flow of seepage that emanates from transitions between rock layers where groundwater collects. On these walls, hanging gardens of luscious green mosses provide a backdrop to elegant groves of cinnamon fern and dense thickets of ninebark.

Near Rockwood, the Casselman quiets again, and is generally silent for a time. Downstream of the town of Markleton, the gradient steepens, and the river again growls a deeper song. Along this stretch, the river takes a more southwesterly direction, hugging the west flank of Negro Mountain. It is cutting across the foundation layers of rock, and in places, running into resistance. The river tries to makes a turn to the west, but intervening geology prevents the change in direction, and the water takes a broad turn and swings back flowing nearly east, back toward the continental divide.

The laws of nature and physics prohibit uphill flow, so the Casselman works its way around a peninsula, or hogback ridge in a striking loop that turns south, southwest, west, and then finally back to the original northwest direction. In this short distance, the water changes direction by almost 360 degrees. The Youghiogheny at Ohiopyle duplicates the same feat, only on a larger scale.

Through the loop the Casselman shouts, and this is one of the most remote and scenic parts of the Great Allegheny Passage. The railroad, not interested in scenery, took a shortcut here and bored through the neck of the hogback. The cut through the rock is the Pinkerton Tunnel. The tunnel is off limits to you as a trail visitor, but the detour is far from inconvenient. The mile and a half bypass trail is a delightful path following the swing of the river through mature woodlands. In the summer, the river is just out of visual reach, but in the leafless seasons, the grand vista opens. In the Pinkerton Loop, the river drops sixty feet in two miles. The bridge on the north side of the Pinkerton Tunnel is just above the surface the water. The bridge on the southwest side is high above the rapid water. The high view provides a panorama of the river and the rapids below. It is also a graphic example of just how steep the gradient of the Casselman, or any river, can be. As a point of reference to the regional geography, at the outer edge of the loop, the Great Allegheny Passage is only about four and a half miles northeast of the 3,218-foot Mount Davis, the highest point in Pennsylvania. However, the loop's peak is only 1,605 feet.

Pinkerton Low Bridge over the Casselman River near Markleton. Photograph by Paul g Wiegman.

From here, the Casselman heads for an appointment with the Youghiogheny River and Laurel Hill Creek in Confluence. The Casselman still sings and sometimes roars on its way to the meeting, but not with the gusto articulated around the Pinkerton Tunnel loop. Confluence is a modern name. The town was once called—officially or unofficially—Turkey Foot. From the Great Allegheny Passage the reason is not apparent; you need a map or a hawk's view to see that it is an appropriate name. From a high vantage point, you would see that at the

base of the eastern side of Laurel Ridge there is a huge imprint, carved by the streams and rivers, of a turkey ambling southward. The Youghiogheny is one toe to the south; the Casselman is the middle toe a little to the southeast; and Laurel Hill Creek is a crooked third toe to the east. Confluence is at the end of Laurel Hill Creek and the Casselman, and their union with the Youghiogheny—thus the modern name. I prefer Turkey Foot.

The Great Allegheny Passage crosses the Casselman for the last

Confluence of the Youghiogheny (in the foreground) and Casselman rivers at Confluence. Photograph by Paul g Wiegman.

time just south of Confluence. At this crossing it is an unremarkable river, vastly unlike the deep, green, still pools between farm fields at Meyersdale, the frothing drops in narrow rapids below Markleton, and the wild swings at the Pinkerton Loop. In the end, the multifaceted Casselman quietly gives up its water to one of the most beautiful, wildest rivers in the eastern United States.

The first introduction to the Youghiogheny is one of slow water just released from confinement beneath the dam south of Confluence. The river is shallow and broad, and its water rolls over cobble, setting the surface to sparkle in the sun. The river seems to be blinking its eyes after being trapped in the dark depths of the reservoir. In a short distance, it is greatly empowered when given the waters of Laurel Creek and the Casselman River.

Just past the meeting of the three waterways, at Ramcat Rapids, the Youghiogheny begins to flex its muscles and wear at the hardness of the sandstone. Ramcat Rapids are a prelude to the kinds of tricks the combination of rocks and rushing water can pull. The story here is short; by the time the water is four miles past Confluence, the river quiets in a broad, shallow flow that includes several islands—features that are not common on the rivers that shadow the Great Allegheny Passage.

The section of the Passage from Confluence to Ohiopyle is, in my estimation, the most scenic. An additional benefit is that it passes entirely through public land, Ohiopyle State Park. A ride on this leg could easily be done in a short time, but there are numerous distractions. The river is close to the Passage, both horizontally and vertically in many places, and the waters seem to ask you to dip a toe or even more. Valley walls to the south are magnificent forests beginning to mature and regain their original pristine composition and grandeur with trees and wildflowers begging to be admired. Steep side valleys mysteriously whisper—"park the bike and come walk for awhile." The ten-mile stretch can take an hour, but it's far more enjoyable if it takes a day.

Nearing Ohiopyle, the Youghiogheny tires of its silence and stretches its watery legs and grumbles at the boulders in its path. The grumble grows to a roar at Ohiopyle Falls, a twenty-foot drop over Pottsville sandstone. Below the falls is an entrance to a run of rapids that twist and turn the river in ever-changing patterns.

The Youghiogheny makes a loop much like the Casselman's loop at the Pinkerton Tunnel, but choreographs the circle dance on a grander scale. As you cross the beautiful new bridge for the Great Allegheny Passage at the north end of town, the Youghiogheny is not far below. The trail follows a gentle curve to another bridge over the river in less than half a mile, across the narrow neck of the Ferncliff Peninsula Natural

Spring trees between Confluence and Ohiopyle. Photograph by Paul g Wiegman.

Area. To reach the second, and much higher, bridge, the river follows a path of nearly two miles and drops nearly seventy feet. The high bridge at Ohiopyle demonstrates the steep gradient of the river, but it is also another of the highlights of the Great Allegheny Passage. The views up and down river are grand. Railroad Rapids is in sight from the upstream side of the bridge. Boaters, professional and novice, negotiate the ragged path of the water between jagged boulders—some displaying skill, and some who spend considerable time hung up on chunks of

Pottsville sandstone. After the rafts exit the rapids, they lazily drift under the bridge looking like little toy boats. Downstream, the view is of the sheer walls of the river gorge. Here is a stunning testament to the erosive energy of the river and the eons it has taken to cut through the resistant layers of the folded Allegheny Mountains.

The trail downstream of Ohiopyle is more about forests, rock cliffs, and side valleys than about the river. The Passage is now well above the level of the water, and it takes some bushwhacking and climbing down—and back up—steep slopes to touch the water. But the river never lets you forget it is there. The rapids that are found along this part of the course generate a roar that filters up through the trees to the trail. Usually the drone is punctuated by the yelps, hollers, and shrieks of rafters confirming their triumphs or calamities.

Often a stop along the Passage and a short hike up one of the trib-

Railroad Rapids on the Youghiogheny River downstream from Ohiopyle. Photograph by Paul g Wiegman.

Sugar Run Falls just off the trail in Ohiopyle State Park. Photograph by Paul g Wiegman.

utary valleys provide a chance to enjoy some of the small waterfalls of the region. Sugar Run Falls is easily reached by a short trail that leads from the Great Allegheny Passage to the base of the falls. The trail is found on the south side, a short distance after Bottle of Wine Rapids. Just before the trail to Sugar Run Falls is another trail up the valley of Jonathan Run. Both of these cascades are best visited in the spring when water is abundant. Bruner Run marks the end of the most popular run for rafts and kayaks. From there, the din of the river quiets as it passes through the depth of the Chestnut Ridge water gap. The Youghiogheny here repeats the broad, shallow character it exhibited when it passed through Laurel Ridge.

Finally, the river broadens, deepens, and quietly leaves the Allegheny Mountains and heads into its final stretch to a meeting with the Monongahela. First the water has to pass through Connellsville where it is confined by bulkheaded banks. After the urban restrictions, the Youghiogheny again glides through a nature-dominated valley with generously wooded slopes. The mighty rapids of the mountains are replaced by shallow riffles with the cobbled bottom close to the surface. Between the riffles are long stretches of still, deepwater pools. Canoes and small boats with whispering fisherman floating in silent pools replace earsplitting rafters cascading through rapids. The floodplain of the river is wider, and the trail is often a considerable distance from the water, but the Youghiogheny sometimes reappears from behind a curtain of silver maples and sycamore. Where the flood plain is broader and flatter, towns and villages have grown.

Just before the bridge at Boston, the free-flowing Youghiogheny melds with a calm pool of nearly motionless water. Powerboats replace canoes, and muddy banks replace rocky ledges. At McKeesport, the Youghiogheny quietly gives its collective waters, gathered from high elevation swamps, rock glistening seeps, silver thread rivulets, and tumbling mountain streams, to the Monongahela River.

For the fifteen miles from McKeesport to Pittsburgh, the Monongahela is less a river and more two long, narrow, lakes separated by a single dam eleven miles upstream of the Point. The edges of the river are mostly artificial walls of steel or concrete, interspersed with welcome patches of naturally sloping floodplain, which gradually descend into the river and support shady groves of silver maple and sycamore.

Riffle in the otherwise placid Youghiogheny River, near the former Banning Mine #4, upstream from West Newton. Photograph by Paul g Wiegman.

Motorboats are bigger and mixed with massive working barges moving coal and chemicals up and down the river.

The Monongahela is a far cry from the wild waters of the Casselman or the Youghiogheny, but the urban river has a majesty of its own. It has a broad channel and a regally slow flow of water that parades past steel, concrete, and glass manmade structures. The river seems to remember that it carved these valleys; it brought the sediment to sculpt wide, flat benches along its shore; it provided the space for men to build dwellings and places of commerce; and it is proud of the achievement. The Mon is especially regal as it approaches the center of Pittsburgh, passes under the Hot Metal and Birmingham bridges, and joins the Ohio on its trip to the center of the continent.

For the length of the Great Allegheny Passage, trees are your constant companions. From the southern born and bred redbud along the slopes of Jennings Creek that tumble toward Cumberland, to the sugar maple venerated with its own festival in Meyersdale, trees line the length of the Great Allegheny Passage. From the young tulip poplars queued beside the trail at Ohiopyle, to the tree-of-heaven desperately clinging to a rare patch of soil in the shadow of Pittsburgh buildings; from a single red maple in a Buena Vista backyard to the grand forests of the Youghiogheny Gorge, trees provide perches for May's migrating warblers and award you shade from August's blistering sun. Eastern North America is a land of forests. To ride the length of the Great Allegheny Passage is to pass through several major forest communities that dominate the eastern United States. The forests set the world along the Passage ablaze in October with a multihued spectacle jacketing the rugged landscape. In winter, they make the sun flicker like a strobe light as you ride through tree trunk shadows that stretch across the trail and are reminiscent of the ties that once lined the path.

From Cumberland to Pittsburgh, the Great Allegheny Passage traverses a variety of landscapes and climatic regions. The diversity of trees reflects the different lands and climates. The generalized forest types described here represent both what was in the past, and what will be. They are the forests that blanketed this region prior to settlement, and they are forests that will return if nature is allowed its own course.

The Passage is a transect that begins in the woodlands of the south; touches, at its highest elevations, northern communities more common to New York and beyond; plunges into the protected valleys of the Casselman and Youghiogheny, which again have forests of the south; and finally, in the Monongahela Valley, showcases woodlands typical of the Pittsburgh Plateau Province.

Hot Metal Bridge crossing the Monongahela River in Pittsburgh. Photograph by Paul g Wiegman.

Paw-paw tree flowers near Cumberland. Photograph by Paul g Wiegman.

The deep valleys around Cumberland encompass the northern edge of southern woodlands. Here, oaks, hickory, and pines clothe the lower slopes of Wills and Haystack mountains and cross over to the east flank of Big Savage Mountain. These are dry woodlands, growing in the rain shadow of the looming Allegheny Front to the west. In the poor, gravelly soils alongside the trail, post oaks display their distinctive crucifix-shaped leaves. They are at the very northern limit of their range, and along with Virginia pine, various hickories, and pitch pine, present to the westbound traveler a last glimpse of the woodlands that dominate the Potomac Basin.

After the long climb up the eastern face of Allegheny Front and into the higher elevations, the trees along the Passage are northern hardwoods adapted to the colder and moister climate. Woodlands of this type are a southern extension of forests more prevalent in northern Pennsylvania and beyond. The American beech, black cherry, sweet birch, northern red oak, and scatterings of white pine and eastern hemlock flourish in the climate of the elevated Allegheny Mountains.

Just past the town of Rockwood, there is a good representative of this type of forest community. The woodlands are composed of stately hemlocks along with typical deciduous species. This grove gives you a brief glimpse of the grandeur of the mountain forests that existed before settlement and wholesale removal of pristine forests. Beyond the quiet dignity of the trees, the Casselman noisily vies for attention with a rush of rapids hidden behind the dark line of rhododendrons next to the river.

Descending from the highlands into the gorge of the Youghiogheny River, another forest shades your ride. Here, on the deep protective walls of the water gaps along Laurel and Chestnut ridges, the Great Allegheny Passage cuts along the bottom of rich, moist, north-facing slopes clothed with one of the most diverse temperate forests on earth. This woodland community is the centerpiece of the Appalachians. Labeled mixed mesophytic forest by ecologists, and commonly called cove hardwoods, it reaches its grandest examples further south. The hallmarks of cove hardwoods are the wide array of species that are a part of the community and the deep, rich soils on which it thrives. In a small, sheltered cove on a north-facing mountain slope, there may be as many as thirty species of trees.

Even here in the Youghiogheny Gorge, at the northern limit of range for the cove hardwoods, the diversity of trees is impressive. The maples are here—red, sugar, and mountain. White, red, black, and scarlet oaks grow in various niches. American beech stands along with basswood, white ash, cucumber tree, box elder, yellow birch, black birch, black cherry, black walnut, shagbark hickory, and sourgum. Even the evergreens make an appearance in the form of scattered eastern hemlock and white pine.

A sample of this distinctively Appalachian woodland is found be-

Mixed forest near Rockwood.
Photograph by Paul g Wiegman.

tween Confluence and Ohiopyle, within the state park. Although not pristine, the rich wooded slopes are recovering from the gluttony of logging during the late 1800s. During the late 1800s and into the early 1900s, the uplands, slopes, and river bottoms in the area where the passage now runs were denuded of trees. Photographs from the period show the nearly complete lack of forest—only a few spindly trunks remained in a landscape of severed limbs as trees were cut down for lumber, chemicals, mine posts, and assorted other goods that fueled a growing human expansion. Today, the new woodlands, left undisturbed, are slowly regaining their quiet majesty. Yellow, or more aptly called tulip, poplar is often the first tree to begin a new forest after logging or other disturbances have ceased. Its seedlings grow rapidly in full sun, and once it becomes a full-grown tree, the tulip poplar is imposing. A rapid grower, the trunks reach straight for the sky like an arrow. The bole expands, building a massive column topped with a dense crown of light green leaves. On the slopes of the Casselman and the Youghiogheny, if you were able to count the rings of many of these trees, you would find that they all had pretty much the same number of concentric circles, somewhere around 100. They all started life after the cutting of the original forests.

Smaller tulip poplars along the trail mark an even more recent change. Downstream of the high bridge at Ohiopyle, the trail is lined with young trees, all of the same size. These are the seedlings that started when the Western Maryland Railroad stopped corridor management. While the trains still ran, the old right-of-way was regularly cut, burned, or otherwise cleared of vegetation. Trees that tried to thrive in the light were kept at bay. Once the management stopped, the tulip poplars took over with abandon. Now the fast-growing young trees can be seen along the side of the trail, and mark the change from steel wheels to rubber tires and hiking boots.

Just over four miles from Confluence,

Yellow poplar flower near Buena Vista. Photograph by Paul g Wiegman.

the trail and river are at the deepest part of the Laurel Ridge water gap. Along the way there are tributary valleys that dissect the face of the gorge and scalloped coves where forests are maturing. Here, all the forest parts come together—trees support a high, verdant canopy; small saplings and shrubs grow in the deep green shade and build a lower canopy; and slope-hugging thickets and wildflowers spread a carpet of color on the forest floor that changes with the seasons. It is a rare visitor that is not tempted to lean one's bike against a tree and take off on foot to explore along the tumbling streams that carved these small valleys and imagine oneself to be the first person to witness the majesty and mystery of these woodland places.

Cove hardwoods are slowly returning throughout most of the Youghiogheny Gorge from Confluence to Connellsville. In the lower Youghiogheny Valley, there are other patches scattered on north-facing slopes, including a beautiful remnant grove at the southern end of Cedar Creek Park in Westmoreland County. The diversity of tree species present in the cove hardwoods is especially evident in autumn. Each species has its own distinctive color. At the peak of fall, the Youghiogheny Gorge is a crazy quilt of yellow, scarlet, purple, red, gold, russet, and other hues with names concocted by imaginative interior designers.

Connellsville marks the trail's exit from the Allegheny Mountains and is the gateway to the Pittsburgh Plateau Province, where one encounters another forest type. The river valley is not as deep here and, in places, forests typical of the uplands cascade down the valley slopes, but Appalachian oak forest or mixed oak forest is dominant here. As the name implies, this is a gathering of oaks. White and northern red oaks are common, and the woodlands include scarlet, scrub, chestnut, and black oaks, along with sugar maple, sweet birch, assorted hickories, and occasional scattered white pines.

☙

If the woodlands present a thrilling richness of color in the fall, spring brings the colors of neotropical migrants who use the low water gaps to avoid flying over the mountains. Along the length of the Great Allegheny Passage, birds punctuate the vegetation and are an added pleasure for the traveler. Warblers are the highlight of early May as they search for insects among the unfolding leaves, but the Passage is also home to orioles, rose-breasted grosbeaks, scarlet tanagers, indigo buntings, and vireos, which mix with the resident black-capped chickadees, blue jays, tufted titmice, and nuthatches.

Once migrants from the south are settled in and have found a home, one species is as ubiquitous as the trees. The red-eyed vireo is probably the most common bird along the length of the Great Allegheny Passage. Although seldom seen, it is constantly heard. It is a small, pale olive bird of the treetops that can be found perched on an upper branch, usually after considerable searching with binoculars. Its song tumbles from the treetops from when it first arrives in the spring, through the June breeding season, and even beyond into midsummer, when it vies with the cicadas for aural attention. Few other birds are as relentless singers as the red-eyed vireo. The males have an idiosyncratic short song with an inflection that seems to be asking a question. For those interested in experiencing the greatest avian pleasure, the simple rule is to get going early—early in the season and early in the morning.

The forests are home to a variety of wildlife in addition to birds. When you travel around a bend, a gathering of deer may be having a morning meal alongside the trail where the vegetation is short and ten-

Autumn in the Youghiogheny River Water Gap between Confluence and Ohiopyle. Photograph by Paul g Wiegman.

der. Evening travels are also likely to provide a glimpse of these common creatures.

An even more common sight is the scurrying of little brown, black-striped bullets as they scamper across the path. Chipmunks are simply everywhere along the Great Allegheny Passage, whether in the wildness of the Casselman or Youghiogheny valleys or passing through villages and town parks. Sometimes it seems as if the chipmunks have made a game out of seeing who can dart across the trail in front of bikes without getting a flattened tail.

On rare occasions, you may come across a raccoon; opossum; red or gray fox; gray, red, or fox squirrel; or, on very rare occasions, a black bear. As the sun gets higher in the mornings, especially in the spring after the night has been particularly cool, snakes use the trail to warm up their cold-blooded bodies. The most common are garter and black snakes.

Many of the animals that once resided here have been lost to the logging of the late 1800s and early 1900s. Permanently lost from the region of the Great Allegheny Passage are the buffalo, passenger pigeon, and the Carolina parakeet, which had previously roamed the woodlands and filled the skies.

The woods are even quieter now due to habitat changes and forest fragmentation that have affected the homes and breeding habits of songbirds. Fortunately, the Great Allegheny Passage provides the impetus to maintain a core of public lands covered with unbroken forests. In these forests we can still listen to wood thrushes, ovenbirds, and great horned owls calling between the valley walls.

As you travel the Great Allegheny Passage, the details of your surroundings smudge and become a continuous sweep of green. Occasionally you should—no, I would say you must—stop and revel in the details. What you will find are the wildflowers that populate the forest floor, species that are even more diverse than the forests and trees.

Wildflowers grace the trail along its whole length. They may be a rarity, such as Carolina tassel-rue in the crevices of the scoured rocks lining the Youghiogheny around Ohiopyle, or as common as goldenrod squeezing its way up through the rubble remains of Eliza Furnace just a few miles from the Point in Pittsburgh.

Wildflower season on the Great Allegheny Passage extends from April to October, but even in the other months, the remnant fruits, pods, seed heads, and other reminders of the growing season are abundant and a challenge to the observant eye. Added bonuses for the wildflower enthusiast are the changes in trail elevation. They translate to being able to see the same seasonal highlight again and again just by cycling a different part of the trail at a different elevation. If you miss the show of trillium, trout lilies, and toothworts at Cedar Creek Park in Westmoreland County, you only need to head into the mountains of Somerset County and enjoy a similar display where Lick Run joins the

Tree frog near Pinkerton Horn, Somerset County. Photograph by Paul g Wiegman.

Tiger swallowtail butterfly on Turk's cap lily in Ohiopyle State Park. Photograph by Paul g Wiegman.

Casselman, or along the Great Gorge Trail leading from the west end of the high bridge at Ohiopyle.

The Passage's great variety of landscapes provides countless opportunities to enjoy the wildflowers of the region. As the trail winds the serpentine valleys, it is constantly changing direction. Although for the most part you are either generally going to the northwest or southeast, at one time or another, you are traveling toward every point of the compass—north, south, east and west. Likewise, the valley walls alongside face a variety of directions. The sun at this latitude is always in the southern sky. In the winter, the sun is lower and in the summer higher, but always shining from the south. Valley walls facing south are baked by direct sun. In the winter this melts snow more rapidly and less water soaks into the soil. In the spring, when the trees are without leaves, the soil is bare and loses even more moisture, creating a relatively dry environment. North-facing valley slopes, on the other hand, never see the harsh face of the sun. The light and heat skim the slopes, allowing the snows to linger and slowly release water into the soil. In the leafless spring, the warming rays reach emerging wildflowers, but do not bake moisture from the soil. These sun-sheltered slopes are native wildflower gardens that give the Great Allegheny Passage some of its most beautiful venues. They are the places where the bike wheels need to rest and bikers' senses need to be flushed of the constant crunch of tire on limestone and hum of chain on sprocket. They are the places to listen to the song of a warbler, see the crisp whiteness of a trillium, and feel the delicate leaf texture of squirrel corn.

Riding the trail in April through May requires that you keep one eye on the compass and the other on the slopes on either side of you. Around the bend, the trail may swing west and glide by a north-facing slope covered with beds of red and white trillium, Dutchman's breeches, toothworts, wild ginger, violets of blue and yellow and white, spring beauties, blue phlox, jack-in-the-pulpit, and a host of other wildlings. These slopes are ideal for the identifier who wants to spend hours poring over field guides to make sure he or she knows what wildflowers are in view. The slopes are scattered along the trail unevenly, so that every turn ahead leads to the anticipation of a new garden of wildflowers. They are idyllic for the photographer intent on capturing the essence of spring. And they are perfect for the dreamer who sits and imbibes the pleasure of a warm spring day, a myriad of color, the sound of a rushing river nearby, and the hum of nature.

Later in the season, where early trillium had carpeted the woodland slopes, jewelweed now fills in with red-speckled, orange flowers hanging under broad leaves. These spotted flower gems offer nectar to

*Snow trillium at
Cedar Creek Park,
Westmoreland County.
Photograph by Paul g
Wiegman.*

hungry insects and iridescent hummingbirds. Where wild blue phlox
flowered, wild geranium follows with its own brand of blue. Where early
meadow rue enjoyed the moisture from dripping rocks, cinnamon ferns
stand tall in the moist soil.

Not all the herbaceous plants lining the Great Allegheny Passage
are common inhabitants. In the Youghiogheny Gorge, the trail follows
the river that was born in highlands to the south. The waters picked
up seeds and other plant parts and carried them to new localities further north. This is the way plants, without apparent means of self-
locomotion, travel. The deep gorge protects the river from the brunt of
winter, and the water further ameliorates the microclimate of the deep,
sheltered water gaps. A little bit of the southern Appalachians' climate
exists in a narrow strip along the course of the Youghiogheny River
through the Allegheny Mountains.

*Dutchman's breeches,
early spring, near
Harnedsville. Photograph
by Paul g Wiegman*

Habitat for the southern-born plants is provided in miniature wet-lands that fill cracks in the sandstone beside the river. In addition, on the river edges, the rush of the water and the debris carried by the wa-ter whittle away at woody vegetation until it is carved down to ground level. This cleansing of the river edges creates the open, sunny habi-tat preferred by several plant species that are adapted to moisture-filled crevices.

One of these species is Barbara's buttons or marshallia. This stately purple member of the aster family looks like an overgrown, garden-variety bachelor button. It blooms in early June in a number of patches along the Youghiogheny from Confluence to Connellsville. The best place to see marshallia is at Ohiopyle. A stop at the south end of the low bridge, just beyond the restored train station, is a good place to start a walk onto the rock ledges between the trail bridge and the highway bridge. The open bare rock steps are prime marshallia habitat. With a little bit of looking, you will find small colonies of this rarity scattered about the area. Like marshallia, the Carolina tassel-rue is characteristic of a southern biome that reaches its northern limit of range in Pennsylvania. The tassel-rue is broad, lettuce-like leaves and tall stalks topped with bright white clusters of small, tubular flowers, grows in wet soil within sight of water.

Late summer is another peak for wildflowers. Along the streams, in the unfarmed open meadows along the trail, and indeed along the edges of the trail itself, the flowers of August abound. Goldenrods, sunflowers, joe-pye weeds, bonesets, and white snakeroots line the path waiting to be noticed. These are plants that have been growing throughout the season and have reserved their show for the end. Like the slope wildlings, the sun-loving summer flowers have their own spaces, and those spaces are dotted all along the Great Allegheny Passage.

If anything except seasons separates these two distinct groups of flowers, it is their proximity to humans. The spring bloomers are distant, away from human haunts. They are part of wildness, of maturing forest, of places only lightly touched by human hands. The flowers of late summer fill gaps left by people. Goldenrods gather in fields once reserved for corn. The sunflowers are the first to voluntarily brighten abandoned factory grounds, and the joe-pye weeds edge the ditches that carry water on new paths away from the trail.

A story of the Great Allegheny Passage would not be complete without some note of the great rhododendron. Common where there is shade and moisture, this grand evergreen becomes as familiar to a rider as the trees. Every month of the year it adds a touch of green to the landscape. In late June or early July it contrasts the dark green with the brilliant white of its flowers.

Every year is not a spectacular year for the shrub. Some years the

Marshallia, an endangered plant in Pennsylvania, along the Youghiogheny River at Ohiopyle. Photograph by Paul g Wiegman.

Butterfly weed near Frostburg, Maryland. Photograph by Paul g Wiegman.

flowers are small and sparse. In other years, the big, robust plants that cling tenaciously to moist rocky slopes and line sections of the creeks, streams, and rivers are awash with white, and the glory of the blooms is breathtaking. Regular riders on the Great Allegheny Passage should take note of the places where the rhododendron are abundant and then wait for that just-right year for an unforgettable ride on a July day.

Great Allegheny Passage at P&LE mile marker 29, Blythedale.

Along the trail between Connellsville and McKeesport.

Flat-bedded sedimentary rock on the Pittsburgh Plateau between Connellsville and McKeesport.

(right) Bridge over Wheeler Flats near Connellsville.

Trail through Connellsville.

Cyclist entering Connellsville from the north.

Remains of beehive coke ovens near Adelaide.

"THE BEST PASSAGE THROUGH THE MOUNTAINS"

Braddock's Road in the War for Empire, 1752–1758

MARTIN WEST

The origin of the celebrated Braddock's Road, which linked the Potomac and Ohio river watersheds to become a vital part of the future Great Allegheny Passage, can be traced to a decision made by a Virginia land speculation company in 1752. At that time, an overland route was planned through the Allegheny Mountains to the Ohio River Valley to increase trade with the indigenous peoples and effect colonization. The British, represented by the Virginians, used the trading path for an unsuccessful diplomatic mission to the French in northwestern Pennsylvania in 1753. As a primitive military road, it enabled Virginian and British troops to advance into the disputed territory and challenge the French in armed encounters in 1754. A year later, a greatly improved road allowed for the transport of heavy siege artillery by the British, but it also led their army to a shocking defeat by a numerically inferior French and Native American force on the banks of the Monongahela River. By 1756, the clash for empire between the two contending powers became global, extending from the waters of the Ohio to the Ganges, the Rhine, and beyond. The conflict, which became known as the War for Empire, the French and Indian War, or the Seven Years' War, concluded in 1763 with a complete British triumph. The long imperial struggle between France and Great Britain in North America had finally come to an end.

During the seventeenth century, the upper Ohio Valley had been occupied by such cultures as the Allegheny Iroquois, the Erie, the Monongahela, and the Mahoning. The "Beaver Wars," a series of destructive conflicts among the indigenous nations, in combination with disease and migration, had reduced and dispersed their populations by 1700. The Delawares probably entered the region shortly thereafter, and the Shawnees, who had a socially fragmented history and apparently never resided in a single community, also relocated at this time, some settling with the Delawares. By the early 1740s, elements of the Iroquois Confederacy or Six Nations (Mohawk, Oneida, Onondaga, Cayuga, Seneca, and Tuscarora), claimants to the Ohio Country by right of conquest in the Beaver Wars, sought a physical separation from their enemies and, lured by new hunting grounds with the opportunity to trade with the French on Lake Erie, moved from New York to what is today western Pennsylvania. Most of these migrants were Senecas and Cayugas, the western-most Iroquois, and became known as the Mingoes. When the War for Empire began a decade later, the western extension of the Great Allegheny Passage, which generally corresponds with the course of Braddock's Road, was a nexus of trade and hunting, especially in the region of the Forks of the Ohio, where a cluster of settlements, large and small, was concentrated.

The central cause of hostilities in the 1750s was the question of dominion in the Ohio Country, a vast zone south of Lake Erie extend-

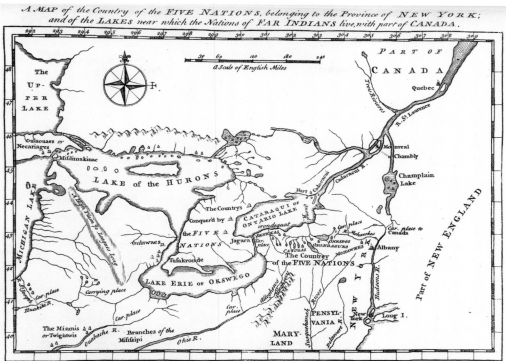

A MAP of the Country of the FIVE NATIONS, belonging to the Province of NEW YORK; and of the LAKES near which the Nations of FAR INDIANS live, with part of CANADA.

N.B. The Tuscaroras are now reckon'd a sixth Nation, & live between the Onondagues & Oneidos; & the Necariages of Misilimakinac were received to be the seventh Nation at Albany, May 30th 1723; at their own desire, 80 Men of that Nation being present besides Women & children. The chief Trade with the far Indians is at the Onondagues rivers mouth where they must all pass to go towards Canada.

ing from the French *Pays des Illinois* (Illinois Country) in the southwest to the Allegheny River in the northeast. The region incorporated the upper reaches of the Ohio River—the great waterway formed at the confluence of the Allegheny and Monongahela rivers—and the strategic point known as the Forks of the Ohio (modern-day Pittsburgh). Although the scene of international conflict, the Ohio Country also should be regarded as a multicultural frontier, involving not only the

"A Map of the Country of the Five Nations." From Cadwallader Colden's History, London, 1750.

French, Canadians, British, Virginians, Marylanders, and Pennsylvanians, but also the "Ohio Indians," the Mingoes, Delawares, and Shawnees. Far from being marginal auxiliaries of the European kingdoms and their North American colonies, the Ohio native peoples pursued a sophisticated policy of self-interest to protect their lands. A Mingo leader, Tanaghrisson, perceptively referred to the Ohio region as "a Country between."

The question of European title to the Ohio Valley had been in contention for several decades prior to the outbreak of the Seven Years' War in 1754. The French asserted that *La Belle Rivière*, their name for the Ohio River, belonged to them due to the explorations of René-Robert Cavelier de La Salle in 1669–1670. Their intention was to dominate the rich fur trade and to secure the physical connections to, and thus the interests of, the two immense North American provinces of France, Canada in the north and Louisiana in the south.

British claims were based on the legalism that the region was embraced by the royal charter granted in 1609 to Virginia and reinforced in 1744 by the Treaty of Lancaster, which was negotiated between representatives of Virginia, Maryland, Pennsylvania, and the Iroquois. By acknowledging royal authority throughout Virginia with its ill-defined western borders, the Six Nations, the colonists argued, also conceded dominion of the Ohio Country to Britain. In the king's name, Virginia Lieutenant Governor Sir William Gooch was directed in March 1749 to cede two hundred thousand acres of western lands between the Allegheny Mountains and the Ohio River to the Ohio Company of Virginia, a firm consisting of wealthy and influential Virginia leaders and planters. Included in the transfer were instructions to colonize one hundred families in the great tract, with the expectation that the profitable western fur trade would be secured and fostered to British advantage. In addition, the company was empowered to negotiate with the Ohio peoples and to erect fortified storehouses within the confines of the land grant.

The Ohio Company of Virginia, which made the path that would become Braddock's Road and later the Great Allegheny Passage, thus sought profits in land speculation, the deerskin trade, and colonial settlement in the Ohio Country. It quickly authorized construction of two strong trading posts to protect its new holdings. The first, the headquarters, was built immediately across from the confluence of Wills Creek and the north branch of the Potomac River on the Virginia side. Fort Cumberland (present Cumberland, Maryland) was later erected on the Maryland riverbank, opposite the depot, providing a western portal while furnishing a refuge for settlers and pro-British natives. The company planned a secondary storehouse, soon to be called Redstone, to be located sixty miles to the northwest, across the mountainous divide between the Potomac and Ohio rivers, where Redstone Creek emptied into the Monongahela (near today's Brownsville, Pennsylvania).

A line of communication was needed to connect the two depots, and the company engaged Christopher Gist, trader and surveyor, to explore west as far as the Great Miami River (in present western Ohio). From 1751 to 1753, he traveled from the Potomac to the Monongahela and Great Kanawha (in present West Virginia) rivers on a system of existing trading routes, which aligned in part with the passage later to be called Nemacolin's Path, after the Delaware scout associated with Gist through the fur trade. The path was mapped and established during the late summer of 1752 as the most direct route possible, corresponding with Gist's November 1751 trip from the Potomac to the Monongahela, which was several miles less than the track previously followed by Virginia traders to the west. Starting at Wills Creek, Nemacolin's

Path proceeded over three succeeding mountains—Wills, Savage, and Meadow—to arrive at Little Crossings (near modern-day Grantsville, Maryland) on the Youghiogheny River. It crossed Negro Mountain, continuing through the ford at Great Crossing (later Somerfield, Pennsylvania) on the upper Youghiogheny, to climb Briery Mountain and arrive at a small, marshy valley called Great Meadows (eleven miles southeast of present Uniontown, Pennsylvania). There, the footpath progressed in a northwesterly direction across Laurel Hill (later called Mount Braddock), and descended to arrive at Redstone Creek, which led to Redstone on the Monongahela River. At Laurel Hill, another trail, the old Ohio Traders' Path, split from Nemacolin's Path and continued on to the Forks of the Ohio. As a result, the new Nemacolin's Path extended northwest from Wills Creek to Laurel Hill to terminate at Redstone on the Monongahela. Much of the eastern segment of this trail, as well as part of the Ohio Traders' Path, would be integrated into Braddock's Road three years later.

In June 1752, Virginia and Pennsylvania commissioners negotiated a treaty at Logstown (near present-day Ambridge, Pennsylvania) with the Mingoes, Delawares, and Shawnees to ratify the 1744 Treaty of Lancaster by the Six Nations. The goal of the colonists, who distributed £1,100 worth of presents to encourage native favor, was to initiate settlement in the upper Ohio Valley, beginning at the confluence of the Allegheny and Monongahela rivers. The Mingo leader Tanaghrisson, fearing the French, asked the Ohio Company to construct a fortified trading post similar to the one on Wills Creek at the Forks of the Ohio. As a result, permission was granted not only to fortify this strategic point, but also the right of Virginians to colonize east and south of the Ohio River was recognized by the Six Nations, and acknowledged by the Shawnee and the Delawares.

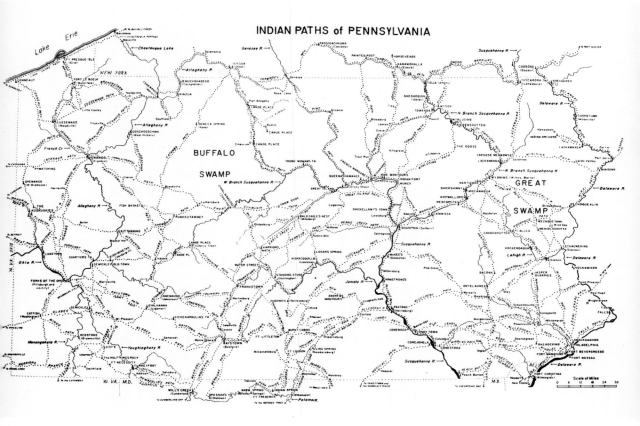

French designs on the Ohio Valley were substantiated by the action of the governor of New France, Roland-Michel Barrin, comte de la Galissonnière, who had reinforced the national claim on the disputed region by authorizing a mission in 1749 under Captain Pierre-Joseph Céleron de Blainville to gauge rising pro-British sentiment in the Ohio Country. In October 1753, Lieutenant Governor Robert Dinwiddie of Virginia commissioned an eager George Washington, a surveyor and

"Indian Paths of Pennsylvania." Almost all early roads in this country followed Indian trails. Courtesy Library and Archives Division, Sen. John Heinz History Center.

"THE BEST PASSAGE THROUGH THE MOUNTAINS" 81

militia major, to carry a summons to the French in occupation of two new posts, Fort Machault (now Franklin, Pennsylvania) at the joining of French Creek and the Allegheny River, and Fort de la Rivière au Boeuf (present Waterford, Pennsylvania) on French Creek. Washington was to demand their immediate evacuation and establish the authority of His Majesty King George II over lands claimed by Virginia. In the event of a rejection, London had authorized "force of arms" to press its claim.

On October 31, Washington set off, soon to be accompanied by his guide, Christopher Gist, and five others. From Wills Creek, Washington's party followed Nemacolin's Path as far as Laurel Hill, where it turned onto the Ohio Traders' Path, to pass by the Forks of the Ohio and reach nearby Logstown. When the party arrived at Fort Machault on December 4, 1753, Captain Philippe Thomas Chabert de Joncaire refused the summons, directing Washington north to Fort de la Rivière au Boeuf. On December 11, the major presented to the commandant of the latter post, Captain Jacques Legardeur de Saint Pierre, Dinwiddie's message, which asked, in part, "by whose Authority and Instructions you have lately marched from *Canada*, with an armed Force, and invaded the King of *Great-Britain's* Territories . . . it becomes my Duty to require your peaceable Departure." Diplomatically, the captain responded, "As to the Summons you send me to retire, I do not think myself obliged to obey it." Unsuccessful in his mission, Washington returned to Virginia in early January 1754, a round-trip of almost one thousand miles.

Already concerned by the arrival of French troops in the Ohio Country, Dinwiddie became more alarmed when Washington informed him of their increasing activity in western Pennsylvania to defend the proposed fort at the Forks of the Ohio. Heavy ordnance from

George Washington in the uniform of a Virginia militia colonel. Painting by Charles Wilson Peale. Original in the Washington-Curtis-Lee Collection, Washington and Lee University.

Britain had arrived in Alexandria, Virginia, which was near the head of navigation on the Potomac. Dinwiddie also called for a coordinated defense against the French. Entreaties to the governors of the other colonies proved only partially effective; unregimented, independent companies of the British army from South Carolina and New York were committed, and Dinwiddie's own House of Burgesses appropriated £10,000 for recruiting the new Virginia Regiment. He also authorized Captain William Trent, an Ohio Company agent and veteran colonial officer, to raise one hundred Virginia militiamen and proceed west "to

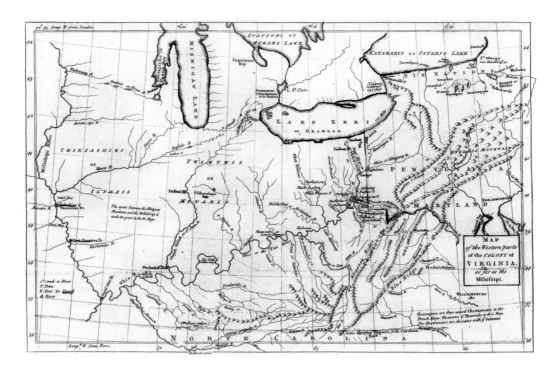

"Map of the Western parts of the Colony of Virginia," including western Pennsylvania and Maryland. From George Washington's published Journal, 1754.

annoy the Enemy." Trent complied and was subsequently at Redstone on the Monongahela in February 1754, superintending the building of the storehouse, when he received new orders from the lieutenant governor to move downriver to the Forks of the Ohio and begin construction of a stockade there.

Commissioned lieutenant colonel and deputy commander of the Virginia Regiment by Dinwiddie in late March, Washington left Alexandria on April 2 with several companies. On arrival at Wills Creek, he learned that in Trent's absence, the French had seized the unfinished fort at the Forks on April 17. After a hurried war council, the Virginian, intending to reach Redstone and fortify Trent's storehouse, embarked on Nemacolin's Path while simultaneously opening it into a crude road to move the heavy artillery to be sent from Virginia under command of regimental colonel Joshua Fry. Advised that the French were building Fort Duquesne at the Forks of the Ohio, Washington left Wills Creek on April 30. On May 9, he reported to Dinwiddie that instead of "light expeditious Marches" on Nemacolin's Path, he was encountering problems:

I detach'd a party of 60 Men to make and amend the Road, which party since the 25th of Ap[ri]l, and the main body since the 1st Inst[an]t [of May] have been laboriously employ'd, and have got no further than these Meadows ab[ou]t 20 Miles from the new Store [at Wills Creek]; where we have been two Days making a Bridge across and are not gone yet: The great difficulty and labour that it requires to amend and alter the Roads, prevents our March[in]g above 2, 3, or 4 Miles a Day, and I fear (tho[ugh] no diligen[ce] shall be neglected) we shall be detain[e]d some considerable time before it can be made good for the Carriage[s] of the Artillery with Colo[nel]. Fry.

By May 24, the Virginians had followed the path fifty miles west to Great Meadows and pitched camp. On the morning of May 28, Washington and Tanaghrisson led a detachment that ambushed a small, unsuspecting French contingent above a rocky glen in a skirmish of fifteen minutes. Ten of the surprised party were slain, including Ensign Joseph Coulon de Villiers de Jumonville, the French emissary sent to demand that Washington remove his troops. One was wounded and twenty-one captured; one escaped. Of Washington's men, one was killed and two or three were wounded. The French survivor reported to the commandant at Fort Duquesne that Jumonville was delivering his diplomatic summons to Washington when, without provocation, he was murdered by a fusillade of small arms. Dinwiddie would later blame Tanaghrisson and his Mingoes for the incident. Although the facts are in dispute, the musketry at what became known as Jumonville Glen is credited with igniting the Seven Years' War.

Washington realized that the French would surely return in considerable strength. Beginning May 30 at Great Meadows, a short distance from Nemacolin's Path, the Virginians erected a small, circular palisade, two-thirds of it covered by shallow trenches, which they completed on June 3 and referred to as Fort Necessity (near present-day Farmington, Pennsylvania). The prospect of French retaliation presented Tanaghrisson with no alternative but to stay temporarily with

Fort Duquesne. Map by Robert Stobo, 1754.

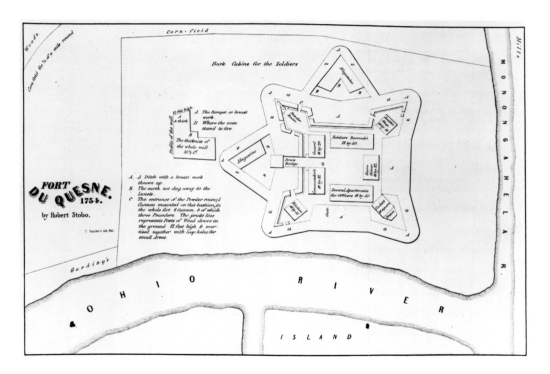

Fort Necessity. Drawing by Charles Morse Stotz. The reconstructed fort is operated by the National Park Service and open to the public. Courtesy Library and Archives Division, Sen. John Heinz History Center.

the British. In early June he and about eighty Mingoes were encamped at Great Meadows, but did not engage with either side. The Ohio peoples distrusted both European contenders, and, accordingly, some departed the region while others decided to await the course of events.

Six days later, Joshua Fry's reinforcements arrived, but without their colonel, who had died on May 31 of injuries suffered in a riding accident. Sole command of the Virginia Regiment now devolved upon the twenty-two-year-old George Washington. Insufficient wagons and the poor condition of the new road being opened on Nemacolin's Path meant that Dinwiddie's ten heavy cannons had not yet reached Washington. More reinforcements arrived in mid-June, as the regulars of the Third Independent Company of South Carolina under Captain James

Mackay gave the colonel approximately three hundred rank and file. Leaving Mackay in charge of Fort Necessity, Washington and most of his men traveled toward Redstone, attempting to widen the route for Dinwiddie's heavy artillery, but they were thwarted by Nemacolin's Path, as Washington explained: "our Wagons breaking very often." Washington left a small party toiling on the road while moving most of his men to Gist's plantation (near present-day Mount Braddock, Pennsylvania), settled by the Ohio Company in 1753, to ascertain the whereabouts of the French.

Washington had cause for concern. The late Jumonville's elder brother, Captain Louis Coulon de Villiers, had embarked with about five hundred French and two hundred Ottawas and Wyandots from the Great Lakes, accompanied by a small number of Ohio warriors, and proceeded up the Monongahela Valley in pursuit of Washington. Washington received word of the French mobilization at Fort Duquesne and, convinced that no other course was feasible, he led his soldiers the thirteen miles back to Fort Necessity over what the colonel described as a "hilly Road form'd Naturally for Ambushes." Their fatigued condition, combined with the poor road and lack of carriages, prevented further withdrawal, necessitating a stand.

Word soon arrived that the French had reached Redstone, and then on July 3, Villiers, following Nemacolin's Path from Redstone and having viewed the glen where his brother died and the remains of several unburied countrymen, arrived before Fort Necessity. An opposing sentinel discharged a swivel gun, and the French returned fire from small arms at long range. The defenders sallied from the fort to deploy in formal line of battle because Washington expected a conventional engagement, but his adversaries closed to sixty yards and opened fire from the forest. In a driving rain, the Virginian and his men withdrew to their fortifications as the concealed attackers continued a heavy musketry, sporadically answered by the partially exposed garrison. By dusk, Washington had suffered over one hundred casualties, while Villiers had sustained only three dead and seventeen wounded. Although the French were short on powder and ball, and their native allies had grown restive, the heavy losses suffered by the British, their inferior numbers, low provisions, and the flooded condition of their fort rendered surrender inevitable.

In the absence of a formal state of hostilities, that night Villiers offered Washington a capitulation in which the British were to withdraw immediately and peaceably to their own territory, with the French captain's promise that their safety was guaranteed against molestation by his warriors to the extent possible. The surrendering men were allowed to remove all of their possessions save the artillery. Honors of war were granted, permitting the garrison to march from Fort Necessity with drums beating and one swivel gun retained. With all the draft animals killed by the attackers, arrangements were made for a cache of British effects to be retrieved later under arms, with the proviso that no other fortifications be made at the Great Meadows or elsewhere west of the mountains. The French demanded that every prisoner taken May 28 at the Jumonville ambush be expeditiously released to the safety of Fort Duquesne; as a guarantee for this last article, two Virginia captains, Robert Stobo and Jacob Van Braam, were to be detained as hostages for a maximum of seventy-five days. In the process of reading aloud the instrument of surrender, Washington's interpreter, Van Braam, a Dutchman, inadvertently mistranslated two key French words, causing the Virginian to confess unwittingly to the "murder" of Jumonville, which led to international outrage.

The surrender of Fort Necessity in July 1754 prompted the careful and deliberate organization in Great Britain of a special expeditionary corps, led by Major General Edward Braddock, age sixty, to build a road to Fort Duquesne in order to take the post. Born in London, Braddock rose to lieutenant colonel of the elite British Coldstream Guards Regiment in 1735 and served in the War of the Austrian Succession (1740–1748), largely in an administrative capacity. Acting governor of Gibraltar for a brief tenure, Braddock was promoted to major general in March 1754 and received his fateful trans-Atlantic assignment the following September. He was regarded as a capable administrator and a strict disciplinarian, who was politically trustworthy.

Braddock's charge was to cut a road across the Alleghenies, seize Fort Duquesne, and then move north against the enemy-held posts on French Creek and the eastern Great Lakes. Minimal regard had been given to logistics and geography in North America. Fort Cumberland in western Maryland, Braddock's expected forward support base, was more than one hundred miles from the Forks of the Ohio, too far, as was to be proved, to serve as haven in the case of a reversal.

Major General Edward Braddock.

Braddock's weaponry and stores were shipped in late 1754 and transported overland from Alexandria to Wills Creek in May of the following year. The officer responsible to Braddock for building the vital new road to the Forks of the Ohio was the deputy quartermaster general in North America, Sir John St. Clair. St. Clair, a Highland Scot, had been a British officer in the Low Countries and Minorca during the War of the Austrian Succession. His responsibilities on

Fort Cumberland. Drawing by Charles Stotz. The site of the fort is now totally occupied by the city of Cumberland. Courtesy Library and Archives Division, Sen. John Heinz History Center.

the Ohio expedition included reconnaissance, provisioning, quartering troops, and road building.

Braddock himself reached Virginia by late February 1755 and discovered that distances on a map in London neither conformed to the physical geography encountered on the North American continent nor disclosed the hardships involved in conveying a European army with siege capacity across terrain without roads. St. Clair commented that what was considered in England "as easy is our most difficult point to surmount, I mean the passage of this vast tract of Mountains." Searching for alternatives, the general concluded his famous transaction with Benjamin Franklin, whereby Pennsylvania agreed to triple the support train with a supply of 150 civilian farm wagons, teams, and drivers and to provide 1,500 packhorses.

The building of Braddock's Road, an approximate 115-mile route, proved a daunting engineering challenge. Wherever feasible, St. Clair followed the route of Nemacolin's Path from Wills Creek to Great Meadows, and from there used the Ohio Traders' Path almost to the Forks of the Ohio. In so doing, his working parties encountered rivers and streams, thick undergrowth, towering hardwoods, wetlands, steep grades, and massive rock outcrops. The worst obstacles were avoided by going around them, but St. Clair attempted to minimize the numbers and lengths of such detours. Another major problem was the lack of forage for the numerous horses and livestock.

Braddock's army contained various artisans, artificers, and armorers essential to campaigning in North America, as well as the wheelwrights, blacksmiths, bridge builders, saddlers, and tanners necessary for road construction. Everything needed for this strenuous effort was carried in the convoy. A variety of entrenching tools issued by St. Clair to his workers included felling axes, pickaxes, saws, shovels, spades, chisels, wedges, hatchets, billhooks, fascine knives, wheelbarrows, and handbarrows. Since the cutting implements demanded frequent sharpening and regrinding, supplies also included files, grindstones, and whetstones.

Upon completion, Braddock's Road was about twelve feet in width, which enabled the various wagons, carts, limbers, and artillery pieces to pass in single file. The only surfacing it received was the filling of holes, minimal grading of knolls and hillocks, and the displacement of large rocks. Troops did not remove stumps of felled trees due to the time and toil involved; the beds of wagons and carts initially could pass over them without contact, although due to erosion, jagged, projecting

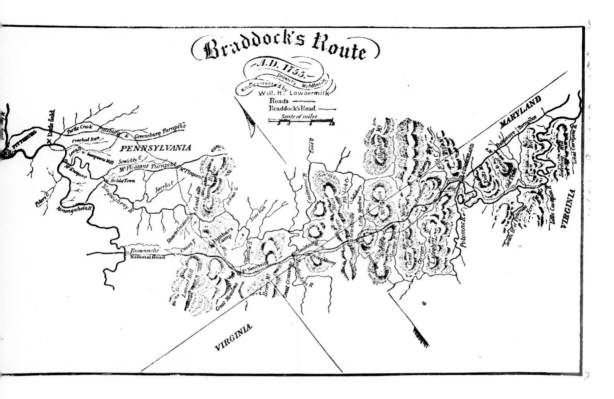

Braddock's Route, 1755. Drawing by Middleton, corrected by Will. H. Lowdermilk.

stumps sometimes broke axles or upset vehicles. In an exception to the normal surfacing procedure, the men sometimes completed a "corduroy," which involved the close, parallel placement of heavy logs across the road for a short distance to provide a stable bed in low, marshy areas.

On the morning of June 18, road cutters under the indefatigable St. Clair left Little Meadows, with Braddock's division following the next day. The general's progress remained slow, leading Washington to remark wryly of Braddock's and St. Clair's efforts that, rather than "pushing on with vigour, without regarding a little rough Road, they were halting to Level every Mold Hill, & to erect Bridges over every brook." Washington, who had been crestfallen to learn that Braddock had been authorized to offer qualified candidates nothing more than captains' commissions by brevet in the British regulars, had accepted the role of extra aide-de-camp, hoping to gain distinction in action and eventually receive preferment from the general in the form of a field officer's commission in the king's land service. Upon leaving the camp at Georges Creek (near modern-day Frostburg, Maryland) on June 14, Washington, ill with fever, continued on with the advanced division that had departed Little Meadows five days later. By the time they had arrived at Bear Camp (near present-day Oakton, Maryland) on June 23, the indisposed Virginian remained behind while Braddock entered Pennsylvania. Washington did not recover sufficiently to join the general's advanced flying column until July 8.

On the July 9, the British troops, nearing their goal, crossed the Monongahela (present Braddock, Pennsylvania) a mere six miles from Fort Duquesne. Confident and almost jubilant in anticipation of victory, and having met no opposition thus far, the colorful military host, parading along the new road to the fifes and drums playing "The Grenadiers' March," temporarily relaxed its usual vigilance. At about one o'clock, the three hundred troops at the head of the column, led by Major Thomas Gage, were astonished to find themselves confronting an equally startled enemy. The British instantly fired. The French commander, Captain Daniel-Hyacinthe-Marie Liénard de Beaujeu, in the act of deploying his men, was killed in the third volley. His deputy, Captain Jean-Daniel Dumas, quickly signaled 637 warriors, 146 Canadian militia, 72 colonial marine infantry, and 34 officers and cadets to fan out and disappear. They enclosed both sides of the road, flanking and ultimately almost surrounding their foe.

Minutes later, the British vanguard panicked and retreated, abandoning two 6-pounders and a supporting ammunition wagon, only to collide with Braddock's main body, which had incautiously rushed forward in response to the sound of the guns. Immediately behind Gage with the road builders, St. Clair was struck by a bullet in the shoulder. Organization disintegrated as the shocked soldiers, ignoring their officers' orders and exhortations, but too fearful to shoot and move against a nimble, concealed adversary, thronged together under appalling fire in a narrow corridor approximately 250 yards in length. Before abandoning the field, the Redcoats suffered about eight hundred casualties in a fight of over three hours against opponents screened by trees and occupying a dominating height. The French losses were apparently less than fifty. Washington, mounted on horseback like the other staff and field officers, received bullets through his hat and coat, but was not injured. Shot through the lungs in the final phase of the engagement, Braddock was not as fortunate.

Recrossing the Monongahela River (near present-day Kennywood Park, West Mifflin, Pennsylvania), the remnants of the vanquished flying column fled along the road the forty miles back to Colonel Thomas Dunbar's camp (near present-day Hopwood, Pennsylvania, on the grounds of the Jumonville Christian Camp and Retreat Center), not far from the burnt timbers of Fort Necessity. Carried there in the jolting bed of a covered cart, Braddock finally succumbed to his wound on July 13. The die-hard Englishman, witness to the rout of his command, was said to have uttered in rueful disbelief "who would have thought it," and added prophetically before expiring, "we shall better know how to deal with them another time." To protect his remains, Washington directed that the general be buried inconspicuously beneath the road that bore his name (indicated today by the Braddock Grave Marker). Having no recourse to a depot, by August 1755 the shattered and demoralized army, now under Colonel Dunbar, had destroyed massive stocks of arms, ammunition, and supplies, and fled the hundreds of miles to Philadelphia and winter quarters.

Various reasons have been offered to explain the defeat of British regulars at the hands of an outnumbered, outgunned, and unconventional force. Braddock fought according to what proved to be inappropriate European principles of warfare, and yet neglected standard tactical doctrine of the day. He was an inflexible and incompetent martinet, and several surviving officers implied that the enlisted men panicked in the battle. Contemptuous of the indigenous inhabitants of the region, he spurned and insulted them, thereby losing the support of the Ohio nations. Regardless of the relative merit of these and other arguments made then and later, undeniable was the tactical superiority of Braddock's opposition at the Monongahela on July 9, 1755. The debacle shocked the thirteen colonies, damaging the settlers' faith in the British military and creating a great fear of the skilled native fighting men, who were sustained by the French in the expanding border conflict. Although much maligned, Braddock, nonetheless, had successfully opened a new road in the backcountry.

In 1756 and the year following, major British military operations in America shifted northward, leaving Pennsylvania, Maryland, and Virginia largely undefended and vulnerable to violent enemy incursions, a manner of unconventional fighting known as *petite guerre.* Such small-scale but effective combat was characterized by mobile groups of warriors, who harassed their foe, soldier and civilian alike. War parties, occasionally accompanied by French officers, would strike suddenly, burning dwellings, slaughtering livestock, and sometimes killing and scalping their victims. Men, women, and children were often seized to replenish dwindling populations. By 1757, this hit-and-run raiding had destroyed hundreds of structures, creating a swath of ruin across the backcountry. Washington, colonel of a restructured Virginia Regiment, made his headquarters at Fort Loudoun in Winchester, Virginia. From there and from a line of small stockades that extended south, he futilely attempted to defend the long Virginia border against *petite guerre*. The abandoned Braddock's Road, which had cost the British so much in treasure, time, industry, and blood, now only served as a warpath for their enemies.

As the year 1758 began, Washington was optimistic that newly appointed General John Forbes would succeed where Braddock had failed. Forbes had been promoted to brigadier general for America by the Secretary of State for the Southern Department, William Pitt the Elder, with instructions from London to secure the frontiers from Pennsylvania to the Carolinas, which led to the capture of Fort Duquesne. Washington knew that many of the problems encountered three years earlier arose from the protracted, toilsome effort to build the road. In his opinion, were Forbes to take the Braddock route, with a command three times the size of the 1755 army, he could successfully march on Fort Duquesne using a virtually completed road, which merely required light clearing. The campaign of 1758, however, would be Forbes's last; suffering intensely from an unidentified, but mortal illness, he was obliged to be carried on a litter between two horses. His poor health during that year led him increasingly to depend on Lieutenant Colonel Henry Bouquet, a Swiss mercenary with battle experience, who had served in the armies of Piedmont-Sardinia and the Netherlands.

In the spring of 1758, Forbes established a seat of operations in Philadelphia in order to draw on local resources and from the prolific granary that was southeastern Pennsylvania. The Scottish general derived his offensive plan from a European strategy, the "protected advance," a deliberate, methodical expedition through hostile territory, consolidating forward movements by building a chain of posts and supply bases at appropriate intervals. Forbes utilized existing, or erected new, substantial forts approximately every forty miles as he moved on Fort Duquesne.

By June, resentment arose between Pennsylvania and Virginia on the question of the route west; soldiers of each colony were reluctant even to enter the other's province. The Virginians, as with the Pennsylvanians, believed that whichever road was taken to the Forks would eventually become the commercial highway to the west. Forbes, cognizant of their motives, proposed to Bouquet the fresh plan of ignoring Fort Cumberland and Braddock's Road altogether to proceed directly from Raystown (now Bedford, Pennsylvania) to Fort Duquesne. The Swiss colonel agreed, noting that a new road would save many miles of travel, avoid hazardous river crossings, and mislead the French as to the axis of advance. Sir John St. Clair was the first to suggest to Forbes the option of using a rough road from 1755, extending from the Susquehanna River past Raystown.

General John Forbes,
c. 1751.

Henry Bouquet.

Charged by Braddock to provide communication with Pennsylvania, provincial Colonel James Burd had cleared but never completed this passage. Forbes could reach Braddock's route by way of the Burd Road, and then open a new way south the thirty miles to Fort Cumberland, or he could follow Burd's Road for twenty miles beyond Raystown and then complete it to Great Crossing, where a junction with Braddock's Road could be made. On May 7, Forbes authorized fortifying Raystown and reconnoitering Burd's Road and beyond to Great Crossing. Meanwhile, St. Clair reversed his position on Burd's unfinished route in favor of Braddock's Road, greatly irritating the general, who informed Bouquet on July 6 that "Sir John is led by passions." Four days later, Forbes reported to Pitt that he hoped to discover "a better way over the Alleganey Mountains, than that . . . which Gen[era]l. Braddock took," adding that were he to follow the latter, it would "save but little labour, as that road is now a brushwood, by the sprouts from the old stumps, which must be cut down and made proper for Carriages, as well as any other Passage that we must attempt."

When informed of Forbes's consideration of an alternative, Washington, the leading proponent of Braddock's Road, was aghast. To him, the idea of another route defied logic. Regardless of objections, on July 25, 1758, Forbes rendered his final decision: by following the east-west Raystown Traders' Path, the new "road over the Allegany mountains and the Laurel Ridge will be found practicable for Carriages . . . shortening the march about seventy miles besides the advantage of having no rivers to pass." As a precaution, he enjoined Washington to clear away a short portion of Braddock's Road west from Cumberland in the unlikely event it might be needed later, providing what Forbes called "two strings to one Bow."

A frantic Washington arranged a personal interview to dissuade Bouquet from building the new road. After an unsatisfactory conference, the Swiss colonel complained to his general that most of the Virginians could not distinguish the "difference between a party and an army, and find every thing easy which agrees with their ideas, jumping over all the difficulties." Although Bouquet asked Washington to frame his rationale in writing to Forbes, the latter had already resolved to build the new road that would later bear his name.

On August 2, Washington submitted a detailed memorandum, which uncompromisingly mustered all of his arguments in favor of

Braddock's Road while disavowing any private or parochial interests. He indirectly acknowledged a major disadvantage of the old road, however, by proposing that supplies be sent from Raystown through the Raystown Traders' Path to Loyalhanna (now Ligonier, Pennsylvania), which corresponded with the first half of Forbes's proposed road, thence to Saltlick (near present-day New Stanton, Pennsylvania). That same day, in a letter to a friend on Forbes's staff, Washington expressed his anger on paper after meeting Bouquet:

I find him fix[e]d . . . upon leading you a New way to the Ohio; thro[ugh] a Road, every Inch of it to cut, at this advanc[e]d Season, when we have scarce time left to tread the beaten Tract; universally confess[e]d to be the best Passage through the Mountains.

If Colo[nel]. Bouquet succeeds in this point with the General—all is lost!—All is lost by Heavens!—our Enterprize Ruin[e]d; & We stop[pe]d at the Laurel Hill for this Winter—not to gather Laurels. . . . The Southern Indians turn against Us—and these Colonies become desolate by such an Acquisition to the Enemy's Strength.

Establishing a passage to Loyalhanna was a formidable and frustrating task, and Washington would not be silenced. On August 28, he expressed to Bouquet the provoking argument that daunting obstacles would be encountered "in opening a new Road thro[ugh] bad Grounds in a Woody Country" frequented by the enemy, and that had Braddock's Road been used, Fort Duquesne likely would have fallen already. The Virginian's secondary role was to repair the old road for a short distance so as to confuse the French, while the main passage was being cut to Loyalhanna, but an actual linking of the two routes was never to occur.

Washington, idle at Fort Cumberland and growing resentful, finally unburdened himself in a manner that could have caused his dis-

Frontier of Pennsylvania. Map by Nicolas Scull, London, 1775.

missal from the expedition. On September 1, he dispatched a mutinous missive to the Speaker of the Virginia House of Burgesses, John Robinson, explaining that his operations were influenced by "an evil Geni," and that Forbes and Bouquet were "d[upe]s, or something worse to P[enn]s[yl]v[ania]n Artifice—to whose selfish views I attribute the miscarriage of this Expedition." Washington dejectedly predicted that nothing except "a miracle" could save the campaign. He added that much time had been wasted while Fort Duquesne remained weak, losing, possibly forever, a "golden oppertunity" to take the post. He rejected the idea that General Forbes had instructions to construct a new road, and, incredibly, proposed that the matter be taken directly before King George II in London in order to explain this "prostituted" failure. Washington even volunteered to attend a Virginia delegation as aide for this task. The following day, he dispatched a letter with similar pessimistic sentiments to Lieutenant Governor Francis Fauquier of Virginia. Aware that Fauquier was a royal appointee, Washington did not include his outrageous plan to go to England, but forecast that Forbes could not continue beyond Loyalhanna that winter.

Forbes's leading units arrived at Loyalhanna on September 3 under Bouquet to build a fort that would serve as forward base and staging area. Disaster was narrowly averted when, on September 14, a large reconnaissance force, approved by Bouquet and headed by Major James Grant of the First Highland Battalion, was repulsed outside Fort Duquesne. The survivors, by escaping to Loyalhanna, did validate Forbes's strategy of the protected advance. A somewhat similar reconnaissance in force was staged by the French and Great Lakes warriors against Loyalhanna October 12, evolving into a partially successful raid, but the post did not fall. Washington soon reached Loyalhanna, and Forbes and the balance of his command arrived early the following month, their number now totaling five thousand troops. On November 11, the general convened a council of war, and the decision was made to winter there rather than to risk a late-season strike on the Forks of the Ohio. Washington's negative prediction appeared to be valid.

The following day, in a skirmish involving friendly fire that almost cost Washington his life, prisoners divulged that the warriors

Letter from John Forbes to William Pitt, dated January 21, 1759, renaming Fort Duquesne in Pitt's honor.

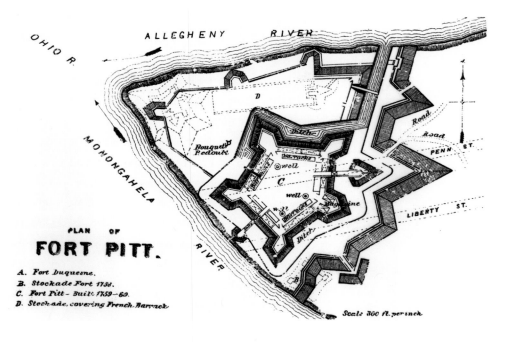

PLAN OF
FORT PITT.

A. *Fort Duquesne.*
B. *Stockade Fort 1758.*
C. *Fort Pitt – Built 1759–69.*
D. *Stockade, covering French Barrack.*

Scale 360 ft. per inch.

Plan of Fort Pitt,
November 1759.

who helped defeat Grant and strike Loyalhanna had returned to their villages for the winter. Only two hundred French garrisoned Fort Duquesne. Forbes immediately countermanded his decision to delay and led a flying column of 2,500 men, a larger number than Braddock's entire force, which opened a rough road on the Raystown Traders' Path, to the Forks of the Ohio. The army was divided into three small brigades, the leading one of which was under Washington, who also prepared the plan of march. On November 25, 1758, Fort Duquesne, detonated and abandoned by the French the previous day, was peaceably occupied by Forbes. The general renamed the site "Pittsburgh," in honor of William Pitt (Fort Pitt was built later); Loyalhanna was designated "Ligonier," after John Louis Ligonier, land military commander in Britain.

Proved wrong in his prognosis of disaster, Washington reported to Fauquier that the capture of Fort Duquesne was a "great surprise to the whole army" and due only to the small number of French, a lack of provisions, and the earlier departure of their allied warriors. Bouquet, on the other hand, maintained that using Braddock's Road "would have been our destruction." The veteran officer understood that Forbes's measured progress on his new road had allowed sufficient time for the British seizure of a vital French supply depot, Fort Frontenac (now Kingston, Ontario), in August of that year, and for the negotiation of the Treaty of Easton, Pennsylvania, in October, key factors in the triumph. Signed by Pennsylvania officials and representatives of the Six Nations and Eastern Delawares, this treaty led many Shawnees and Ohio Delawares to abandon their alliance with France. According to Bouquet, the Treaty of Easton was "the blow which . . . knocked the French in the head."

The French were not only driven from the Forks of the Ohio, they eventually also lost Canada and Louisiana. Great Britain stood victorious in North America and around the world by 1763. When Washington again wore a uniform, it was to lead the thirteen American colonies in their winning struggle for independence from the British empire that he had formerly served. His appointment as commander-in-chief of the Continental army, and his success in that capacity, were largely a result of the experiences between 1753 and 1758 gained on Nemacolin's Path, Braddock's Road, and, although George Washington would not concede the point, the Forbes Road.

Never again would Braddock's Road carry the British troops; it fell

Fort Pitt block house. From Charles Morse Stotz, The Early Architecture of Western
Pennsylvania. *Courtesy Carnegie Library of Pittsburgh.*

into disuse by its builders. Only due to military necessity in 1755, at the beginning of the decisive War for Empire in North America between France and Britain, could this undertaking have been accomplished in such an expeditious manner. For the first time, the Great Allegheny Passage had been opened from the Chesapeake Bay to the headwaters of the Ohio.

Rafting on the Youghiogheny River at Double Hydraulic Rapids.

Double Hydraulic Rapids on Youghiogheny River between Ohiopyle and Bruner Run.

(right) Vista of the Youghiogheny River near Bruner Run Take-Out in Ohiopyle State Park.

Ohiopyle Falls, Ohiopyle State Park.

Winter at Ohiopyle Falls.

Low Bridge over the Youghiogheny River at Ohiopyle.

MIGRATION ON THE PASSAGE

Western Settlement, 1763–1840

JENNIFER FORD

To bike or walk the Great Allegheny Passage is to follow a path similar to that which thousands crossed almost two centuries ago. At the conclusion of the French and Indian War, however, the routes that now make up the Passage sat idle.

When the British finally prevailed over France in 1763, Parliament proclaimed that it had no intention of allowing American colonists into England's newly won territory west of the Allegheny Mountains. Protracted war with France had bankrupted the English treasury, making it impossible to finance military protection for frontier settlements. Moreover, it would have been logistically difficult for colonial authorities along the seaboard to control—and tax—settlers on the far side of the mountains. Thus, Parliament's Proclamation of 1763 reserved the territory west of the Alleghenies for native tribes and forbade American colonists from crossing the mountains in search of land.

In spite of Parliament's "Great Proclamation," hundreds of Virginians and Marylanders walked and rode from Cumberland along Braddock's Road into the mountains of western Maryland and southwestern Pennsylvania. Their numbers included many men who held land grants given to them by the Virginia colonial legislature for militia service. The Monongahela and Ohio valleys were, after all, lands that belonged by royal grant to Virginia. Other ex-servicemen sold their land grants to speculators, men such as George Washington, who purchased vast tracts of acreage and then sent agents to survey their properties and secure their investments.

Unfortunately for the Virginians' plans, native tribes knew that, unlike the French, British colonists intended to clear forests and create permanent farming settlements. To protect their lands and preserve their own way of life, the Delaware, Shawnee, Mingo, and Seneca peoples united to drive the intruders out. In May 1763, warriors attacked settlements from western Maryland and southwestern Pennsylvania to Illinois, inflicting terrible loss of life. In response, Colonel Henry Bouquet marched five hundred British soldiers over the Forbes Road from Philadelphia to Fort Pitt and began to wage war against the native coalition. The British victory at Bushy Run, just east of Pittsburgh, marked a temporary end to tribal resistance in southwestern Pennsylvania.

Settlement resumed after Bouquet's victory. The Penn family purchased land from the Indians at the Treaty of Fort Stanwix in 1768. The treaty moved the boundary, marking native territory far enough west to bring Kentucky and western portions of Pennsylvania and Virginia under provincial jurisdiction. It also signaled the end of England's resolve to limit colonial movement west of the Alleghenies. Anxious to impose some semblance of order on migration, Maryland's colonial governor, Horatio Sharpe, acting on behalf of Lord Baltimore, ordered a survey of western Maryland, and Pennsylvania's colonial government opened

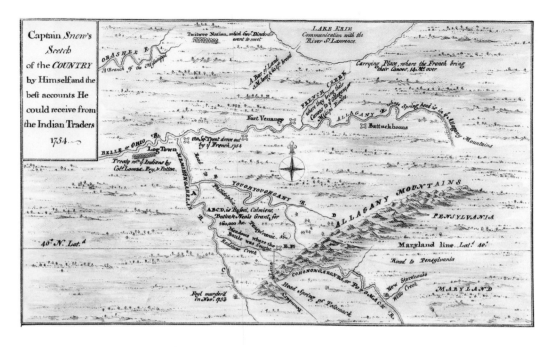

Captain *Snow's Scetch* of the *COUNTRY* by Himself and the best accounts He could receive from the Indian Traders 1754.

"*Captain Snow's Scetch of the Country,*" *1754. The Monongahela and Ohio valleys.*

a land office in 1769 to regulate property sales. While the rugged terrain of mountainous western Maryland allowed only sparse, isolated pockets of settlement, families from Pennsylvania's eastern counties, joined by newly arrived immigrants, set out on the Forbes Road and pushed over the mountains' ridges into southwestern Pennsylvania, where they encountered Virginians and Marylanders coming into the region via Braddock's Road. In 1770, Indian trader George Croghan commented, "What number of families has settled since [Fort Stanwix] I cannot pretend to say positively . . . but last year . . . there were between four and five thousand . . . the roads have been lined with waggons moving to the Ohio."

Henry Bouquet negotiating with the Ohio Indians. From print by Benjamin West. Courtesy Trustees of the National Library of Scotland.

Thus, by the early 1770s, there were a number of important developments in the region: good land open for settlement in the western territory, two relatively good roads leading into the region carved out during the war, and a rapidly growing population. Before long, colonial legislators in Philadelphia had to create a new county—appropriately named Westmoreland—encompassing all of southwestern Pennsylvania. It seemed certain that settlement—the business of taking up land and establishing the economic, political, and cultural hallmarks of western civilization—could now proceed unimpeded. But it was not to be.

The new residents of southwestern Pennsylvania had barely cleared the trees from their fields when they faced danger and dislocation. Over the next two decades, bloody border conflicts with Virginia, war against Britain, and renewed Indian raids slowed permanent settlement long after the process was well underway in other regions.

Just as western Pennsylvania's settlement phase began in earnest, conflict over jurisdiction and ownership in the region erupted between Virginia and Pennsylvania. Each colony's claim had merit. Pennsylvania's original charter, signed in 1681 by King Charles II, had granted all of the disputed territory to William Penn's family. Pennsylvania's legal claim to the land was further strengthened by Parliament in the Stanwix Treaty of 1768. From the southerners' point of view, King George III had granted that territory to Virginia's Ohio Company in 1754. Moreover, Virginia militiamen had shed their blood to oust the French, and settlers with Virginia land grants had been the first into the Monongahela Valley after the French and Indian War ended. The question of which colony held legal dominion over the region simmered for years and finally boiled over in 1773, when Pennsylvania legislators erected Westmoreland County, named Hannastown as the county seat, and installed a court there. In response, Virginia's Governor Lord Dunmore declared Pittsburgh the county seat of the "District of West Augusta," and sent troops to back his proclamation. Suddenly, there were two county seats in the same territory. It was not long before violence erupted over which was in fact the seat of regional jurisprudence.

Leading the Virginia forces was John Connolly, a relative of Governor Dunmore's and an exceedingly ruthless character. During his campaign to oust Pennsylvanians from the region, Connolly's raiders looted and burned homes, shot livestock, even arrested judges and packed them off to Virginia in chains. In April 1774, Connolly galloped into Hannastown at the head of 150 armed men, barred the door to Westmoreland County's log courthouse, and declared that the justices there had no authority to decide cases in the sovereign colony of Virginia.

Thanks to Connolly's raiders, Pennsylvania settlers lived in terror. They were afraid to plant crops, their animals starved or were shot, and there was no local authority capable of providing relief. Hundreds of families simply packed their belongings and left. Those who stayed petitioned the governor of Pennsylvania for assistance. The citizens of Pittsburgh described their situation as "alarming." "Great numbers" of neighbors had deserted, they wrote, and all their own activities were "at a standstill." Help never arrived. Finally, in 1775, a coalition of Pennsylvania settlers banded together and fought back against Connolly. They freed detained Pennsylvanians, and arrested Connolly, who, with his support weakening, was released to return to Virginia, where he embarked upon a new career aiding royalist forces during the American Revolution.

The border dispute between Virginia and Pennsylvania was not legally settled until after the Revolution. In the summer of 1776, however, all residents of the western territory—Marylanders, Pennsylvanians, and Virginians—came together to engage a new enemy: England and its allies, including thousands of Native American warriors. Hostility was so great between American frontier settlers and native peoples that many tribal leaders enthusiastically aided Britain during the War for Independence. Indian raids escalated dramatically during the war, necessitating the fortification of strategically located cabins across the countryside. Neighboring families seeking refuge frequently filled these small "block houses" to capacity. In addition to the constant threat of native raiding parties, wartime demands on manpower and resources further impeded the progress of settlement. In fact, historian George Dallas Albert labeled the early 1780s the "darkest" period in southwestern Pennsylvania's history.

America's victory did little to alleviate suffering in the backcountry. After the War for Independence, native warriors escalated their attacks on the American frontier, hoping to stem the tide of permanent settlement. Many settlers fled the region, and others abandoned their farms and moved close to neighborhood block houses, where armed men stood guard while farmers worked the fields. Such was the case at Hannastown, where a few log buildings circled within a wooden stockade served as the community's fortified refuge.

On a hot July day in 1782, the lookout for a communal reaping party at Hannastown spotted about 150 Indian and "white renegade" warriors approaching the village. The men raced to spread the alarm and gather everyone within the fortified walls. The raiders, upon discovering that their surprise had been foiled, looted and burned the cabins surrounding the stockade. Had the raiders known that the block house defenders had only nine rifles among them, they surely would have overrun the tiny stockade. Instead, a third of their band galloped two-and-a-half miles to a farmstead where the women and young people of Hannastown had gathered for a social event. The raiders descended on the party. They killed or captured everyone, then marched their prisoners back to Hannastown. There, they spent the night drinking, ransacking the smoldering cabin ruins, and torturing their captives within earshot of the block house, where the victims' husbands and fathers remained trapped and helpless. Dawn brought the arrival of heavily armed men from neighboring settlements, and the raiders fled, taking their prisoners. In their wake, they left dozens of people dead or traumatized, and the county seat of Westmoreland in ashes. Hannastown was never rebuilt. Years later Albert interviewed survivors and descendants of the Hannastown raid. According to their accounts, the destruction of Hannastown utterly devastated morale across the region. To many, that terrible day epitomized the never-ending danger and discouragement they encountered while trying to settle southwestern Pennsylvania.

In 1784, two years after the Hannastown raid, Native American elders relinquished all tribal land claims in western Pennsylvania. That same year, the newly minted state of Pennsylvania settled its boundary dispute with Virginia. Although these developments should have encouraged settlement, inflated postwar land prices and the threat of Indian raids continued to hamper development across much of the region for another ten years. In 1789, for example, only approximately 4,800 people resided in the newly established Allegany County of western Maryland. Finally, General Anthony Wayne's 1794 military victory at Fallen Timbers in Ohio ended the threat of attack by Native Americans. When land prices began to decline, southwestern Pennsylvania was at last ready to end its protracted frontier history and begin a true settlement phase.

Thanks to the arrival of new settlers, the population of southwestern Pennsylvania increased steadily after the mid-1790s. Because the region's over-long frontier era ended decades later than in adjacent regions, the new wave of settlers included descendants of American colonists as well as recently arrived European immigrants. By 1800, southwestern Pennsylvania was a patchwork of growing communities settled by families from a wide variety of places. The Great Allegheny Passage crosses townships that were settled by families from Maryland, Virginia, New Jersey, eastern Pennsylvania, Ireland, England, Germany, Scotland, and Wales. The second census of the United States in 1800 recorded just over 100,000 people in the region. In contrast, the smaller area and less hospitable topography of western Maryland had attracted only 7,000 settlers.

The timing of local settlement shaped the demographic makeup of each community. During the dark and dangerous eighteenth century, a few pockets of settlement had flourished in the Monongahela Valley, especially along the Youghiogheny and Monongahela rivers. These communities were established primarily by pioneers who had come into the region via Virginia and Maryland, along the routes of the Passage, rather than eastern Pennsylvania. In the colonial era, Virginia's goal had been to get the wilderness cleared, settled, and on the tax rolls. To that end, the Virginia House of Burgesses set land prices very low, and gave free tracts to immigrants who agreed to settle the property. By the mid-1700s, newcomers were forced to push further and further west and north to find unclaimed land. Braddock's Road and the natural valleys of the Appalachian Ridge funneled settlers directly into southwestern Pennsylvania. Since the Virginia legislators considered that territory to belong to their colony, they granted the land under their customarily liberal terms. As a result, the majority of early settlers in the most southwesterly portions of Pennsylvania had obtained their land from Virginia. Because of them, cultural ties persist between the upland South and parts of Greene, Washington, and Fayette counties to this day. One contemporary wrote in 1772: "Attended a marriage, where all the guests were Virginians. It was a scene of wild and confused merriment. The log house which was large, was filled. They were dancing to the music of fiddle. . . . The manners of the people of Virginia, who have removed into these parts, are different from the presbyterians and germans. They are much addicted to drinking parties, gambling, horse racing & fighting. Several of them, have run through their property in the old settlements, & have sought an asylum in this wilderness."

Settlers from northern Ireland—the Presbyterian "Scots-Irish"—also gained quite a reputation for backcountry fighting, drinking, and merrymaking. While tales of wild Scots-Irish frontiersmen have been enhanced through the generations, the Scots-Irish were indeed the predominant ethnic group in many townships of southwestern Pennsylvania, particularly in Fayette, Washington, and Greene counties and their influence shaped the region into a bedrock of hard work, commerce, and industry.

Families of German descent were also closely identified with early southwestern Pennsylvania. In 1843, gazetteer Charles Trego observed: "A large portion of the population is of German descent, mostly from the eastern counties; and the German language is commonly spoken." As undeveloped land became harder to find in eastern Pennsylvania and Maryland, many German Americans traveled across the Forbes Road into central and southwestern Pennsylvania alongside immigrant families from the German duchies. They composed a substantial majority of settlers in parts of eastern Westmoreland County and in most of Somerset County, where the German cultural influence has remained strong for centuries. More than any other group, German settlers tended to keep to themselves, living and marrying within their own social circles. Their longstanding reputation as exceptionally capable farmers and builders is well supported by most of the region's historical records.

In the twenty-first century, most of us have easy access to paved roads and, therefore, are able to crisscross the mountains in no time. Two hundred years ago, it took weeks to traverse the region on foot or horseback, over old Native American paths or newly cleared roads. In fact, the two major routes into and crossing southwestern Pennsylvania—Forbes Road and Braddock's Road—were little more than rutted paths that soldier-axmen had cleared through the forest in the mid-1700s. In the decades that followed, migrants traveled into and across the region on these crude, narrow dirt paths, which had been chopped through densely forested terrain, over mountain ridges, and into deep valleys. Tree stumps—cut just low enough for wagon beds to clear—stuck up all along the deeply rutted roads, which were often axle-deep in snow or mud. Nevertheless, these dusty, primitive paths provided the best overland routes into and across the backcountry until the early 1800s, when several new "pikes" opened, including the great National Road.

In the early 1800s, the Commonwealth of Pennsylvania began to buy stock in private turnpike companies, enabling those enterprises to build or improve roadways linking the state's towns and markets. The Pennsylvania Road was the longest of these, following the general route of the old Forbes Road and easing the challenge of shipping goods overland between Pittsburgh and Philadelphia. The road was far from perfect or easy to negotiate, but it was a vast improvement over the old trail, and soon laden wagons rolled across the state. Other roads, such as Glades Road and the Huntingdon Pike, were improved as well, but without a doubt the most significant roadway in the region was the National Road, which opened in sections during the 1810s.

Although concerned about overstepping the limits of the federal government, Congress voted in 1806 to underwrite the cost of building a hard-surfaced road that would strengthen the economic and political ties between coastal cities and the western territories. Because soldiers and settlers had used Cumberland, Maryland, as a departure point to the west for decades, Congress chose that town, incorporated in 1787, as the eastern terminus of a great pike that would run all the way to Illinois. The National Road, sometimes called the Cumberland Road or "Old Pike" (now U.S. 40), roughly followed Nemacolin's Path and Braddock's Road before splitting off and going west through Uniontown, Brownsville, and Washington, Pennsylvania, and Wheeling, West Virginia. Although opening a route generally running a few miles west of the Great Allegheny Passage trail itself, the National Road became a key part of the corridor connecting the east and the west. It took enormous amounts of skill, labor, and money, but in 1818, crews finally completed the entire roadway to Wheeling. Although the National Road followed older paths, it represented an enormous improvement over its predecessors. The men who designed and built the road paved it—no more mud and ruts—and built bridges so travelers no longer had to cross through water. Soon thousands were traveling over the wonderful new road by foot, horseback, wagon, and carriage. Many travelers wrote of their delight with the improved route to the west. Uriah Brown, a teacher and surveyor from Baltimore, traveled the road in 1816 and noted in his journal on June 22: "This morning we set out from Cumberland. . . . This great Turnpike road is . . . Masterly Workmanship . . . the Bridge over the . . . Youghegany is positively a Superb Bridge. . . . This [road] . . . will be of more benefit than the Idea of man can possible have any knowledge of."

So many heavy wagons rolled over the National Road that it was soon in need of repairs, not all of which were undertaken in a timely fashion. In 1849, a Mrs. Houstoun noted in her journal that the road between Cumberland and Brownsville was "in a most wretched state—

full of deep holes, deep ruts, and large stones, Fatal accidents are constantly occurring."

Although fraught with their own hazards, the rivers were far more efficient than local roads for moving passengers, household goods, and agricultural or manufactured products over long distances. The Great Allegheny Passage winds through a region that was once a bustling center of boatyards, dotted with embarkation points for travelers on the nation's inland waterways. Philadelphian Joshua Gilpin, while inspecting properties he owned in the region, wrote in 1809: "Families from the eastern parts of the States arrive here, & purchase boats with which they embark . . . the boats they descend in are all of all sorts & sizes some of them being little more than large square tubs with a shed over them—others embark in large Arks . . . & others in keelboats." Even when it was still too dangerous to stay and settle in the region, thousands of westbound settlers began their river journeys here. They set out on the Youghiogheny or the Monongahela river, boating northward to meet the Ohio River at Pittsburgh. The Ohio carried them west, often as far as the Illinois Territory, where travelers could either continue westward or travel south on the Mississippi River.

Many people other than westbound settlers also used the river systems to move goods. When conditions permitted, rafts loaded with western Maryland's agricultural and forest products made the perilous journey down the Potomac River to eastern markets. In contrast, southwestern Pennsylvania farmers rafted their grain, corn, and whiskey over the Ohio to the Mississippi, then south to the seaport of New Orleans. It is hard for us to imagine, but before good roads existed, shipping by river from Pittsburgh to New Orleans—over one thousand miles distant—was easier than hauling bulky goods by packhorse or wagon just three hundred miles overland to Philadelphia.

There were river-going boats for every purpose. Most primitive were the dugouts, so-called because their builders used the Native American method of using fire and chisels to hollow out a large tree trunk to make a canoe. Dugouts ranged in size from lightweight, two-person crafts all the way to fifty-foot behemoths capable of carrying an entire party of settlers with livestock, supplies, and household furnishings. Settlers also transported their possessions westward on large plank rafts called flatboats, which they steered downstream with oar sweeps or pushed upstream using long poles. Most flatboats carried an ark, a room-sized structure in which the travelers ate, slept, and took refuge against the elements. Although some were, as one historian called them, "floating pigsties," others were surprisingly comfortable . . . or at least they seemed so to travelers of the time. In 1787, Mary Dewees journeyed across the Allegheny Mountains to an embarkation point on the Youghiogheny River. After examining her flatboat's interior, she described a space measuring sixteen by twelve feet, "with a Comfortable fire place; our Bed room partitioned off with blankets, and far preferable to the Cabins we met when we crossed the mountains." River travel was not necessarily pleasant or easy, though. The frontier was, after all, usually a rough and ready place, as flatboat man John May quipped: "We allow, at the last computation, twenty souls to a boat, and a great number of bodies without souls." Poorly constructed boats were common, and some boat builders used rotten planks or defective caulking to save on their expenses. Guidebooks of the time cautioned river travelers to have repair kits close at hand. River navigation was a complex art that few bothered to master before they piled their families and possessions onto a flatboat and cast off downriver. There were widely published navigation guides to the rivers, but most men did not develop real boating skills until they had survived several near-

River scene with flatboat and two keelboats. Drawing by Clarence McWilliams for The Planting of Civilization in Western Pennsylvania, *by Solon J. and Elizabeth Hawthorne Buck.*

disastrous encounters with rapids, rocks, storms, sandbars, ice, and the wreckage of other unlucky crafts.

Some local farmers carried their products to nearby river towns and sold them to agents who transported the goods to markets downriver. Others rafted their wheat, whiskey, and lumber downriver themselves. They all found flatboats most useful for transporting goods from southwestern Pennsylvania rivers to the seaport of New Orleans. After the long journey south, many decided against wrestling the heavy flatboats back upstream and sold the vessels for lumber. A farmer in this position could then either buy a horse or save money and walk the one thousand miles back home. Either way, the roundtrip—normally undertaken in late fall and early winter—lasted between three and four adventure-filled months.

Commercial shippers normally owned or hired bateaux, large flatboats that tapered to a point at each end. A well-constructed bateau could carry up to seventy tons of goods such as lumber, iron products, or store merchandise. In the late 1700s, boat builders in the Monongahela Valley began nailing four-inch square beams to the bottoms of bateaux. These beams, or "keels," ran the length of a boat and acted as a protective bumper when the vessels crashed into submerged rocks, an all-too frequent occurrence. Typically sixteen feet wide and up to seventy-five feet long, the keelboats required a skilled helmsman and a crew of oarsmen to navigate downriver. In the early days, the strong-backed oarsmen were often local farmers' sons who wanted to see the world, experience adventure, and earn a bit of pocket money. The various riverboats, despite their risks and limitations, did provide some access to markets for local farmers, both as producers and consumers. In 1803, Thaddeus Harris described this function: "With these [articles] a great many trading boats are laden, which float down the river, stopping at the towns on its banks to vend the articles . . . these trading boats contribute very much to the accommodation of life, by bringing to every man's house the little necessities."

The heyday of commercial flatboats and keelboats had begun to pass by the 1820s, even though floating goods downriver continued for decades. The huge boats were perfect for downstream voyages but getting the vessels back upstream presented a considerable problem. Moreover, the age of steam was about to revolutionize travel and shipping by enabling boats to run fully laden- down *and* upstream. In 1807, inventor Robert Fulton and his business partner Robert Living-

ston made the first successful steamboat trip up the Hudson River in
New York. Quick to see the potential for profit, the two entrepreneurs
established steamboat service from Pittsburgh downriver to the port
of New Orleans. They hired Nicholas Roosevelt (granduncle of Theodore) to oversee the construction of steamboats in Pittsburgh. In 1810,
Roosevelt launched the first steamboat on the western rivers, appropriately named *The New Orleans*. Scottish geographer and merchant
John Melish traveled throughout the United States in the early 1800s.
He was in Pittsburgh in 1810 and saw *The New Orleans* soon after its
launching. He later wrote that it "was the largest vessel I had ever seen
which bore the name of boat." Melish noted that the owners aimed to
have a fleet of steamboats plying the rivers, adding that the plan would
be "of incalculable advantage to the whole western country."

Steamboats were an increasingly common sight on the rivers in southwestern Pennsylvania, and by 1820, the great steamboat age was underway. These large and relatively fast vessels greatly reduced shipping costs and times and vastly increased market opportunities for regional farmers and manufacturers. Seasonal fluctuations in water levels limited navigation every year, even on the Ohio River. Rapids, snags, shoals, sandbars, and ice, along with droughts and annual flooding, made navigation risky, especially on the Youghiogheny River. State and federal governmental efforts to improve navigation on the rivers had little success until the late 1840s. New canals were a late addition to river travel: the Pennsylvania Main Line Canal, terminating at the north end of the Great Allegheny Passage in Pittsburgh, provided commercial movement between Pittsburgh and Philadelphia after 1834, and the Chesapeake and Ohio Canal linked Cumberland with Georgetown after 1853. Together, steamboats, the improved roads and turnpikes, and the new canals made possible the transformation of the region from a self-sufficient, often subsistence-level frontier to a more commercial agrarian economy.

During the initial three decades of the nineteenth century, southwestern Pennsylvania's population doubled, reaching approximately 200,000 in 1830. This represented steady though modest growth, particularly in comparison to the agriculturally superior lands of states north of the Ohio River. Many migrants heading west passed through the region outfitting themselves at Cumberland, Brownsville, Pittsburgh, and Wheeling before continuing their journey. During the next thirty years, due mainly to the cumulative advantages of transportation improvements, the region's population almost doubled again to more than 370,000, with a sizable portion of the growth occurring in Pittsburgh. Even though the basic means and products of farming did

Consolidated Coal Company barge on the C&O Canal, c. 1900. Courtesy C&O Canal National Historical Park.

not change greatly over much of this period, the agricultural communities of the region enjoyed a better standard of living as they became more engaged in the market.

Most settlers of the late eighteenth and early nineteenth centuries came to western Maryland and southwestern Pennsylvania intending to build family farms and farming communities. Normally, their first order of business was to clear trees from a home site and erect a temporary shelter, usually a simple log cabin. Then the family began the back-

FOR SALE,
A Tract of Valuable Land,

SITUATE in Unity township, within one and a half miles of the Loyalhanna, formerly the property of William Maxwell, deceased. containing upwasds of 400 *Acres of good LAND.* o which is a substantial

Log Dwelling House,
a Double Barn and other out buildings, a good Tan Yard and an exerllent Orchard. There are upwards of one hundred acres cleared, a large portion of which is first rate meadow. The Farm is well calculated for raising stock. and has many other advantages which render it very desirable. Persons wishing to view the property and know the terms will please apply to

BENJAMIN ALSWORTH,
Near Hannahstown.

January 23 1819.

Newspaper advertisement selling farmland, January 23, 1819.

breaking business of removing trees, stumps, and rocks from a patch of earth and putting in crops. Occasionally, these newcomers purchased a homestead that had already been partially cleared by a family who had left the area. Their work was eased a bit because they started out with a place to live and a little bit of opened ground. But the primary focus for an entire generation of people who came to the western territory was much the same: to clear land and create farms.

People today tend to say "log cabin" when describing any historic log home. However, the original log dwellings still standing near the Great Allegheny Passage are actually log houses. Authentic settlement-era log cabins were much smaller and cruder than any log house that has survived to the present day. Most pioneer families built a simple cabin when they first arrived; cabins were, in effect, the starter homes of their day. Joshua Gilpin noticed the prevalence of log cabins during his 1809 trip: "In general any person who chuses goes upon the lands he finds vacant & there begins an improvement, by building a house where everything is of logs the chimney not excepted & the roof formed of split pieces like staves . . . this rude shelter . . . frequently has not a particle of iron in its whole composition is the work of a few days and the settlers assist each other." Typically, after a few years on the land during which families cleared trees, planted crops, built a barn, and decided to stay, they erected a proper log house, leaving their cabins to rot or using them for storage or summer kitchens.

Backcountry settlers—sometimes aided by neighbors—usually erected a cabin directly on the ground without any foundation. If the owners bothered with floorboards, they just placed split logs on the ground and then fastened rough-hewn boards called "puncheons" to them. For the cabin walls, axmen felled nearby trees, chopped off their branches, then "bucked" them into logs of roughly the same size. Before they pushed a log up into place, axmen chopped half-moon shaped saddle notches near its two ends so that the natural curve of adjacent logs at right-angles would sit crosswise in the "saddles" above and below and hold the walls together. Since cabins were meant to be temporary dwellings, the men did not spend time or energy hewing the round logs into flat boards with a broadax. Consequently, rainwater tended to flow around and pool between the logs. The result was wood rot and the inevitable collapse of settler-period cabins.

Cabins were usually one-room structures with a few feet of space overhead for a tiny storage or sleeping loft. In southwestern Pennsylva-

Early log cabin. From American Pioneer, *October 1843, reproduced in Charles Morse Stotz,* The Early Architecture of Western Pennsylvania. *Courtesy Carnegie Library of Pittsburgh.*

nia, the average cabin was just eighteen feet wide and sixteen feet deep, barely the size of a modern living room. In this single room, family members slept, cooked, ate, spun yarn, entertained visitors, and stored their clothing, food, and personal items. Cabin roofs—short, ax-split boards held in place by sapling poles—were notorious for providing poor protection from the elements. In June 1798, merchant John May wrote with resigned humor: "Here I am in the wilderness . . . in a log cabin. Through the roof the stars may be studied to great advantage, when the clouds do not interfere."

After they finished the walls and roof, cabin builders simply chopped a rectangular hole—usually in one long side wall—for the door opening. Doors typically consisted of small logs split lengthwise, pegged to cross-battens and secured to the cabin with leather hinges. Axmen created the fireplace by opening a square hole in the bottom of a gable-end wall, then adding a clay-lined firebox and chimney on the wall outside of the opening. A cabin chimney was simply a tall, rectangular box of sticks and clay, built upward and narrowing from the firebox to just above the roofline. Due to the frequency with which wooden chimneys caught fire, builders curved them slightly outward so they would collapse away from the cabin when they inevitably went up in flames. When cabin owners troubled to add a window, they simply cut a small opening, covered it with greased, translucent paper, and outfitted it with a wooden shutter. However, most cabins did not actually need windows for light and air since those elements often flowed right through poorly filled spaces between logs that made up the walls. The chinking materials that filled these spaces consisted of wood chips or stones covered over, or daubed, with varying concoctions of mud, grass, straw, hair, moss, or animal blood. If care was not taken with daubing, wind, rain, snow, and wildlife could freely enter the home.

One settler told of being "snatched partly bald-headed" by a wolf who thrust her paw through an open space in his cabin wall and seized him by the head as he lay sleeping!

Most families who lived in cabins eventually built what they called mansion houses. To our eyes, historic log houses look rather simple, even crude, but in their day they were indeed "mansions," providing many improvements over cabins. The most important characteristic of log houses was square-hewn logs. Squaring off round logs with a heavy broadax was a labor- and time-intensive job, but one which provided important benefits. On the home's exterior, flat surfaces allowed rainwater to run down the walls rather than in between the logs. Square-hewn logs fit together more closely than rounded ones, leaving relatively little space to chink against the elements. To erect a hewn-log house, the builders chopped or chiseled angled notches near each squared log's end, then fitted the notches together to form square, flush corners that provided structural stability. House owners could cover flat-hewn exterior walls with protective "weatherboards" and plaster flat interior walls, thus relieving the brown monotony of log architecture and adding some small measure of refinement.

Stone foundations were the second most important element that log houses had in common. It would have been pointless to hew logs flat and carefully notch them together, then place the house directly on the ground. A stone foundation provided an excellent barrier between log walls and the damp earth; it also raised the house high enough to allow storage space beneath the home. Additional characteristics that log houses sometimes—but not always—included were one-and-a-half or two stories, interior rooms, nailed-on roof shingles, floor joists and milled floorboards, plastered and whitewashed chinking, glass windowpanes, and stone chimneys.

Log house near
Greensburg, built before
1800 (two-story addition
1830). From Charles
Morse Stotz, The Early
Architecture of Western
Pennsylvania. *Courtesy
Carnegie Library of
Pittsburgh.*

Between 85 and 90 percent of southwestern Pennsylvania families lived in log cabins or log houses during the early settlement years. Even by the 1830s, most farmers chose to renovate their log houses rather than replace them with non-log structures. Widespread supplanting of the log house came only after the 1840s, when southwestern Pennsylvania agriculture became more specialized and prosperous.

A few early settlers did build homes with brick, stone, or wood frames. Non-log houses were costly to build; construction materials and skilled craftsmen were scarce and expensive in the backcountry. Well-to-do farm families who built non-log homes tended to prefer

The John Frew stone house in Crafton. From Charles Morse Stotz, The Early Architecture of Western Pennsylvania. *Courtesy Carnegie Library of Pittsburgh.*

stone. Some—usually the most wealthy—erected stone houses immediately; others added stone sections onto their original log houses as time passed and their families grew. The region's brick and wooden frame houses were generally built in large river towns, and were most common in Pittsburgh. The concentration of brick and wooden frame houses in places such as Brownsville, Uniontown, and Washington resulted from both the proximity to sawmills and brickyards and the presence of citizens with the financial means to build them.

In the countryside, farm families often put up sizable barns while they were still living in tiny, ramshackle cabins. This made perfect sense to people whose primary goal was to establish farmsteads. When people think of Pennsylvania barns, they usually picture the imposing structures with overhanging forebays that are common in the south central and eastern parts of the state. However, these distinctive barns were rarely seen west of the Allegheny Mountains before the middle of the nineteenth century. A few large barns—as big as sixty feet by thirty feet—did exist in the backcountry, primarily in Somerset County. Many farmers in Somerset came from eastern Pennsylvania, where two-story frame and stone forebay barns were common, and they built similar structures as soon as they could. However, across southwestern Pennsylvania most settlers originally built simple, one-story log barns. About a third of local farmers in the early 1800s built double barns, at least twice as wide as they were deep. This shape accommodated a center throughway with a section, or bay, on either side. Double barn owners typically stored hay and grain in one bay, sheltered livestock in the other, and used the center throughway as a work space and grain-threshing floor.

After the 1830s, inventors across the nation filed hundreds of new patents on mechanized agricultural equipment, and farmers became more efficient with every passing decade. Before that time, though, farmers generally used the same tools and methods that their fathers and grandfathers had before them. Power came from humans, horses, or water. Tools included a plow, harrow, sickle, scythe, and hoe. The region's forests—especially the oaks, hickories, and maples—provided excellent woods for the various farm tools. Most farmers had scythes, but few had one with a relatively new cradle attachment. The long fingers of a cradle caught the grain stalks that a scythe blade cut, thus eliminating the need for someone—usually women and children—to perform the backbreaking task of picking up the crop after every swing

Newmeyer barn, near Connellsville in Fayette County. From Charles Morse Stotz, The Early Architecture of Western Pennsylvania. *Courtesy Carnegie Library of Pittsburgh.*

of the blade. That task was also dangerous; snakes often bit the hands and arms of harvesters.

The crops that farmers planted across the western territory were much the same in 1830 as they were in the 1790s. Agriculture throughout much of the period was mixed rather than specialized; that is, most families kept a few horses, cows, hogs, and sheep, and raised wheat, corn, oats, hay, flax, and rye rather than specializing in one cash crop. Vegetable gardens were also important, and the forests provided wild fruits, berries, nuts, and meat to augment food supplies. In the early years, when the extent of market participation was minimal, only one-third of the farms had wagons. Many farmers packed their products on horseback to take to nearby merchants.

As the region grew due to more demand, better roads, and many

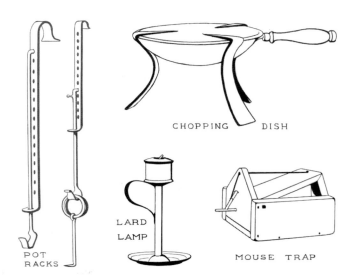

CHOPPING DISH

LARD LAMP

MOUSE TRAP

POT RACKS

Kitchen implements and household implements. Drawings by Clarence McWilliams for The Planting of Civilization in Western Pennsylvania, *by Solon J. and Elizabeth Hawthorne Buck.*

more wagons, an increased number of farmers began to specialize in marketable products. Yet for much of the period, a balanced, self-sustaining mix was the standard. There were a few differences in crop selection across the region based on local climate and cultural preferences. For example, farmers in Somerset planted far less corn than their contemporaries because of their higher elevation and cooler, shorter growing season. They raised more rye than average, however. The county was heavily settled by German families, who preferred rye bread flour, and also had a strong tradition of using rye stalks to weave a wide variety of storage baskets and beehives, or scaps. In the late eighteenth and early nineteenth centuries, farmers across the entire region also used rye as the primary ingredient in whiskey, but it is a myth that every backcountry farmer operated a still. Studies based on tax records and property inventories, rather than traditional lore, reveal that the number of farmers who owned a still was actually about one in ten. There were, however, enough stills in every township to transform everyone's grain into whiskey for local consumption and transport to far-off markets.

Farm families employed several strategies to purchase items that they could not make for themselves, such as iron tools, gunpowder, sugar, or salt. They bartered their labor or farm goods with each other and with local merchants, a very common practice, particularly in cash-poor communities. They took up carpentry, smithing, or coopering, especially during the winter months. Sometimes they rafted surplus products, such as flour, whiskey, and lumber, to Pittsburgh, Louisville, or New Orleans, or packed it on horseback over the Great Allegheny Passage route to Cumberland, then by boat to Washington DC and Baltimore. Women also made butter to sell, especially in regions directly adjoining the Great Allegheny Passage. Farm families of German descent—and there were many in parts of Somerset and Westmoreland counties close to the trail—tended to keep larger dairy herds than the regional average. Their cows also grazed on exceptionally lush pasture land. The happy result was milk high in fat content, perfect for making a rich butter. Moreover, farms in close proximity to the Great Allegheny Passage route had the luxury of access to an overland route to large markets. The road led directly to Cumberland and even further east to Hagerstown and Baltimore, where there was a very strong demand for the famous "Glades" butter of Somerset County.

Many agricultural areas in the southern United States grew and flourished without towns in the vicinity. In the northern states, however, villages and towns were at the economic and cultural heart of most farming communities. In town, a farmer had access to grist-

Somerset County farmstead, 1892. Photograph courtesy George Pyle. Print courtesy Historical and Genealogical Society of Somerset County.

mills and sawmills, blacksmiths and wheelwrights, dry goods merchants, and markets for his products. Farming towns sprang up across the western territory as settlement took root. As late as the Civil War, most of these were small villages with less than three hundred people. Even the county seat towns with extra legal and administration functions had only around five hundred people at midcentury, except for the larger Uniontown located on the National Road. The other larger towns were located on the rivers, where they outfitted migrants, built boats, contained merchants and buying agents so farmers could sell or take products to far-flung markets, and manufactured some goods not available in the villages.

Many towns on or near the Potomac, Monongahela, Youghiogheny, and Ohio rivers were among the earliest and most successful population centers in the region. Cumberland marked the junction of the National Road, the newly opened Baltimore and Ohio Railroad, and the soon-to-be completed Chesapeake and Ohio Canal. It thus connected western Maryland to eastern markets, provided transport services for the many teamsters and boatmen, and outfitted westward-bound travelers. In 1850, this bustling town of more than six thousand inhabitants was the center of urban activity at the eastern edge of the mountains.

Pittsburgh, located west of the mountains, had a population of approximately eighty thousand at midcentury, including the cluster of

One of the earliest mills in western Pennsylvania, completed in 1776, built for George Washington on land he owned in what is now Fayette County. From Charles Morse Stotz, The Early Architecture of Western Pennsylvania. *Courtesy Carnegie Library of Pittsburgh.*

settlements at the Point. This city benefited enormously from its special site at the confluence of the Monongahela and Allegheny and the head of the Ohio rivers. It was the urban heart of southwestern Pennsylvania, offering the most extensive markets, financial resources, and cultural institutions.

Other towns, such as Elizabeth, Monongahela, and Brownsville on the Monongahela River, Connellsville on the Youghiogheny, and McKeesport at the junction of the Youghiogheny with the Monongahela (the latter two along the Great Allegheny Passage route), thrived as river trading points. Joshua Gilpin recognized this when he noted: "The embarkation on the river is not confined to Pittsburgh but takes place on all the towns or ports on the Monongahela." Brownsville, for example, the location of Redstone Fort in the eighteenth century, took its name from Thomas Brown, who purchased land near the fort and began laying out a town in 1785. Brownsville was intended to compete with Pittsburgh and by 1809, as Gilpin described, had become a bustling, important place: "Brownsville united with Bridgeport contains [about] 300 houses & 2000 inhabitants. . . . There are 18 Stores at Brownsville—besides the supply of this immediate country, the river navigation & trade is a great object. . . . The trade of the town on the river consists chiefly of receiving, rafts of logs, wheat flour, whiskey, & a variety of other productions from the upper country which stop here and are exchanged . . . down river." When the planners of the National Road decided to run it through Brownsville rather than Pittsburgh, it caused economic panic among the latter's business community. Until then, the two towns had been well matched in size and development. Pittsburgh, though, soon outstripped its rival farther south on the Monongahela River.

Thus, a network of villages, towns, and one major city emerged in

Pittsburg: Taken from the Salt Worko [sic] two Miles below the City. Lithograph, c. 1850. Courtesy Catherine R. Miller Collection, Special Collections, Jennie King Mellon Library, Chatham University.

the initial half of the century to service the thriving agricultural region. The modernization of agricultural methods and subsequent increased specialization after 1840, the arrival of the railroad at midcentury, and rapid industrialization would soon transform the western territory. The development of its natural resources augmented, and in some cases supplanted, its agricultural focus. Gazetteer Charles Trego, in his 1843 *Pennsylvania Geography*, praised this new energy when he described Brownsville as a "flourishing manufacturing town, and a place of considerable business." Trego was impressed by the town's manufacturing of glass, cotton, rolled iron, paper, and steam engines. Beauty, however, is in the eye of the beholder. Just six years later, traveler and diarist Mrs. Houstoun recalled Brownsville as "a most dirty town, dirty with smoke, and coal, and manufactures."

The redoubtable Mrs. Houstoun may well have been right, but, unlike Charles Trego, she did not venture into the surrounding countryside. There, Trego beheld vistas of great beauty. "Here. embosomed in the dark forest and enclosed between precipitous hills, the foaming river dashes madly over a perpendicular ledge of rock which rises like a wall across the stream, forming a cataract of singular beauty and wildness, whose deep and sullen roar is almost the only sound that is to be heard to disturb the gloomy silence of these solitary woods, or to wake an echo from the surrounding hills." So the magic of the region is revealed. Over the centuries, native peoples, soldiers, traders, settlers, boat builders, road crews, travelers, and manufacturers have passed through, lived along, and left their marks on the Great Allegheny Passage route. What remains for us to appreciate and enjoy is the history of those who came before us and, even more, natural beauty that "the hand of man has yet to destroy."

Long Run along the trail in Ohiopyle State Park.

Ohiopyle from Tharp Knob Overlook in Ohiopyle State Park.

(right) Cucumber Falls in Ohiopyle State Park.

Rider on the Great Allegheny Passage near Ramcat Hollow, Ohiopyle State Park.

Great Allegheny Passage near Ramcat Hollow, Ohiopyle State Park, the first section of the trail built.

Cross-country skiing on the trail near Ohiopyle.

A PASSAGE TO COMMERCE

The Industrial Revolution, 1860–1920

ROBERT GANGEWERE

The waves of commerce and industry that transformed America into an industrial power can be seen today along the Great Allegheny Passage. The route begins at the terminus of the Chesapeake and Ohio (C&O) Canal in Cumberland, Maryland, in a sense a marker of the end of the canal era, and journeys into the heart of the age of coal, iron, and steel—western Maryland and southwestern Pennsylvania—passing through a landscape that is often still as wild and beautiful as it was in the early nineteenth century. This passage from pastoral America into the terrain of coal mining and iron and steel manufacturing has few equals among American trails. It is a route into the history of how the wealth of the land—timber, coal, and iron—was exploited, how manufacturing arose to deliver products to distant markets, and how the people who performed these tasks lived and worked. Railroads through the passage linked these resource activities and industries to metropolitan markets, especially Baltimore and Pittsburgh, and small industrial towns and cities such as Cumberland,

Connellsville, and McKeesport grew to service the industrializing regional economy.

The Great Allegheny Passage is a trail full of signs of historic financial speculation, entrepreneurial thinking, giant corporations, and epic labor struggles. George Washington first traveled it as a soldier in the French and Indian War, and never far from being a plantation owner in need of cash, he speculated in the lands of the region. In later years, the Consolidated Coal Company shaped a good deal of the Maryland end of the Great Allegheny Passage; Henry Clay Frick was the "King of Coke," a material mined in the Connellsville district of southwestern Pennsylvania; and Andrew Carnegie became the "richest man in the world" by building the Carnegie Steel Company in Pittsburgh's mill towns of Duquesne, Braddock, and Homestead. At Homestead, mill workers challenged, and lost to, Carnegie and Frick in the historic strike that changed for decades the relationship between steel workers and mill owners, while numerous labor protests in the mining fields were notoriously contentious and often violent.

Whether traversing the Passage's sylvan beauty or urban landscapes, travelers are never far from the human drama of the industrial age. The trail itself is a legacy of the railroads that were essential to the industrial transformation of the region—a beautiful path through the mountains assembled from the abandoned rights-of-way of three railroads. It allows travelers to glimpse the legacy of the workers and their families who labored in the mills, mines, factories, and rail yards. It passes through, or near, small industrial communities and larger, formerly dense industrial neighborhoods. Company towns, planned wholesale for immigrant laborers in the mines and mills, still dot the countryside, though they are no longer owned by the businesses that built them.

In order to tap the growing western markets of early nineteenth-century America, the merchants of the great eastern seaports—Boston, New York, Philadelphia, and Baltimore—promoted improved transportation routes through the Appalachian Mountains. Concerned that a rival city might gain an advantage, they pursued expansive strategies of building turnpikes, canals, and finally railroads. Once completed, these new routes, despite persistent problems for commercial movement, triggered the exploitation of natural resources and the development of industry along their routes. The Great Allegheny Passage through the mountains was no exception. Baltimore and Pittsburgh markets exerted a powerful influence on the region between Cumberland and the three rivers.

Too far northeast and without proximity to a westward water route, Boston did not have viable commercial access to the nation's interior. The best northern route was from New York. Travelers like Andrew Carnegie's family, just arriving in New York City from Scotland in 1848, steamed up the Hudson River and then went west through a break in the mountains into the Mohawk Valley and on to the Great Lakes via the Erie Canal. At Buffalo, they boarded a steamship and crossed Lake Erie to Cleveland, where they took another canal south to the town of Beaver on the Ohio River, just downstream from Pittsburgh. This roundabout journey took three weeks. Soon the railroads would shorten westward trips over the mountains to a matter of hours, not days.

The middle route westward from Philadelphia led into central Pennsylvania toward Harrisburg and then over the Allegheny Mountains. This path initially involved the Pennsylvania Main Line Canal, completed in 1834, and later the Pennsylvania Railroad, both of which had to negotiate the numerous ridges that had plagued travelers going by wagon. Charles Dickens traveled the Pennsylvania Main Line Canal to Pittsburgh in 1842, sharing cramped, dirty quarters with men who never washed and who spat upon the floor. It was slow going, but he kept his spirits up, and plunged his head in the half-frozen water at 5:30 each morning to wake up. He also engaged in "the fast, brisk walk upon the towing-path, between that time and breakfast, when every vein and artery seemed to tingle with health . . ."

The southernmost of the mid-Atlantic routes over the mountains, favored by merchants in Georgetown and Baltimore, used the Potomac River Valley to penetrate the mountains. Even before 1800, efforts to improve navigation on the Potomac met with little success. In 1806, the federal government authorized construction of the National Road from Cumberland on the river through the mountains to the Ohio River at Wheeling, West Virginia. Sometimes called the Cumberland Road, this improved roadway reached Wheeling in 1818. Nevertheless, in order to keep pace with northern rivals, the C&O Canal was begun at Georgetown in 1828 with plans to reach the Ohio River. Even before reaching Cumberland, the terrain for the C&O Canal presented difficult challenges requiring lift locks, aqueduct bridges, dams, and a long tunnel. Construction was delayed by financial shortages, harsh working conditions, labor riots, epidemics such as cholera, and the high costs of maintaining the operating sections. The canal finally reached Cumberland, 184.5 miles from Georgetown, in 1853, but it was never constructed beyond that point. By this time, Baltimore merchants, left unconnected to the canal, had decided to build a railroad, the Baltimore and Ohio (B&O), which entered Cumberland in 1842 and became an economic rival of the C&O Canal.

Despite the high costs of construction and continual repair, the improvement of commerce resulting from the three interregional canals stimulated considerable economic growth. Of the three, only the C&O

failed to complete a water route to west. The mountains and treacherous waters impeded suitable connections to the Ohio River watershed. The railroad would offer the best possible solution.

Until the railroads traversed the Great Allegheny Passage region after midcentury, most industries, with the exception of some in Pittsburgh and Cumberland, were integral to the local agrarian economy. Farming dominated the regional economy. Flour and grist mills, distilleries, cooperages, and boat building joined traditional artisanal trades like blacksmithing, harness and saddle making, and wagon building in providing crucial services in the processing of farm products. These activities were sometimes scattered across the countryside but also located in villages and small towns.

A few industries developed specifically for nonlocal markets. Logging began to flourish when settlers cleared the land of trees. Well-situated farmers could float logs down the streams to sawmills in many of the region's towns along the major rivers. Boatyards and the towns themselves required lumber; later railroads and mines consumed enormous amounts of timber. East of Laurel Mountain on the Casselman River, for example, the town of Pinkerton once had a sawmill and logging camp. Production there ceased around World War I, and the town no longer exists, but small logging businesses still operate throughout the mountains.

Just as logging was widespread in these early days, so was making whiskey. Farmers had to process grains into smaller bulk products in order to transport them to markets; as a result, whiskey made from rye was nearly universal in the region. Distillers in southwestern Pennsylvania produced a Monongahela rye for local consumption, and it eventually found more distant markets. For many farmers, whiskey was one of their few means to turn some profit.

In order to meet its debts, the new federal government passed an excise tax in 1791 on distilled spirits. The law permitted excise officers, who were to collect cash payment, the power of search and seizure. Distillers and farmers across the western frontier, who believed the distant federal government was failing to solve Native American and land speculation problems, and for whom cash was scarce, engaged in acts of civil disobedience against the law and the tax collectors. Violence broke out in 1794, especially in southwestern Pennsylvania. The small towns of Dawson and West Newton, downstream from Connellsville on the Youghiogheny, were hotbeds of the Whiskey Rebels. Radicals preached insurrection, and a mob threatened to advance on Pittsburgh, a symbol of federal power in the frontier. Respected local citizens such as Albert Gallatin, whose home at Friendship Hill—not far from the Great Allegheny Passage—is a national historic site, moderated the tensions. Nonetheless, President George Washington raised a militia, which he sent to Cumberland. The troops marched from there to southwestern Pennsylvania, met little resistance, and arrested twenty ringleaders from around the region who were carried off to Philadelphia and accused of treason. Most were acquitted due to lack of evidence, and two were sentenced to death by hanging before Washington pardoned them. The federal government had, however, demonstrated its ability to exercise military authority in order to enforce the law and keep the nation intact.

A symbol of the role of whiskey production in the region's nineteenth-century agricultural economy is the Overholt Distillery Museum in West Overton, near Scottdale, Pennsylvania, a few miles from the Great Allegheny Passage. Abraham Overholt, a young Mennonite weaver who "tended loom" in the early nineteenth century, believed whiskey was a product from which a profitable business could be made. By the 1840s, Overholt, Henry Clay Frick's maternal grandfather, had established the family fortune with whiskey making, lumber mills, and gristmills in a rural industrial complex at West Overton. Overholt's Youghiogheny Rye was locally considered the best whiskey, the result of a long-cultivated family tradition in distilling. To expand beyond the local market, Abraham bought out his brother's part of the farm, including the original distillery housed in a log cabin. He erected a new, stone distillery building, eventually making it possible to generate hundreds of gallons of whiskey per day. In 1859, he replaced this distilling facility with a vast, six-story structure. The capacity of the grinding rooms rose to 200 bushels of grain and 860 gallons of "Old Overholt" daily, which he then shipped by wagon, boat, and train to the rest of America. This historic building is now part of the museum complex at West Overton.

Another industry that flourished in the region was glass manufacturing. Roger and Thomas Perry, for example, operated a glassworks in Cumberland in 1816, and in southwestern Pennsylvania, especially, the production of glass thrived. The essential materials for glassmaking were locally available: fuel, silica (sand), and potash (from burning trees and vegetation). A high-quality deposit of silica for glassmaking was discovered at the mouth of Jacob's Creek where it met the Youghiogheny at the boundary of Westmoreland and Fayette counties, and clay able to withstand high heat was available in several places in the region for the pots in which glass was made. Isolated from East Coast glass manufacturers and importers of glassware from western Europe by the mountains, southwestern Pennsylvania had a natural market in towns downriver of the Ohio and Mississippi for glass windows, drinking vessels, bottles, and tableware.

Entrepreneurs established glassworks in southwestern Pennsylva-

Beehive coke oven with Overholt Mill and Distillery in the background. Photograph by Michael D. McCumber. ©2009 mdmPix.com.

nia early on. Albert Gallatin and his partners attracted skilled workers from Maryland and opened their shop in 1797 at New Geneva on the Monongahela River, close to the border of what was then Virginia and is now West Virginia. In the same year, General James O'Hara, who as quartermaster supplied goods to the nation's western armies garrisoned in Pittsburgh, established his glassworks on the south side of the Monongahela River across from that frontier town. These two glassworks initiated an enduring, industrial specialty for the region.

Soon other glassworks followed O'Hara's example, including Bakewell Glass, established in 1808, and also located on the south side of the Monongahela River. Bakewell Glass became famous for its quality and variety. By 1825, four glassworks existed in Pittsburgh and another five in the area south and east of the city. With the rapid growth of the West after 1825, southwestern Pennsylvania's glass industry thrived. In 1837, there were twenty-eight glassworks (fifteen in the city and the remainder nearby), forty-five in 1865, and sixty-one in 1885. Pittsburgh, especially its South Side neighborhood, became the largest glass center in the nation, while several glassworks also existed on the lower Youghiogheny and Monongahela rivers.

Traditional hand blowing and other highly skilled methods of glassmaking remained important parts of the industry throughout the nineteenth century. However, the rapid adoption of innovations, especially in the use of pressed glass machines in the 1870s, led to standardization, faster production, and lower costs, expanding the market for glass products. Skilled machinists, mold makers, and others joined the workforce. The industry's shift to natural gas for fuel, which burned more intensely and cleanly than coal, and increased mechanization in the late nineteenth century spurred a move to much larger

Bakewell, Page, and Bakewell. Engraving, c. 1830. Courtesy Historical Society of Western Pennsylvania.

factories and decentralization from Pittsburgh. By the early twentieth century, plants even further afield where gas was available flourished. Many of the towns where glassmaking boomed, such as Perryopolis, Belle Vernon, and Glassport, Pennsylvania, are located near, if not literally along, the Great Allegheny Passage.

Coal and iron resources continued to add to the region's economy. Settlers had brought iron making, an ancient process, to North America east of the Appalachians in the eighteenth century. The difficulty of transporting heavy iron goods across the mountains to the frontier, however, encouraged the development of iron furnaces farther west, where there was both iron ore and access to acres of forest from which charcoal could be produced for fuel. Iron making before the late nineteenth century relied upon heating iron ore in a blast furnace until it melted and pouring the molten contents of the furnace into molds. When that substance cooled it hardened into what came to be called "pig iron" (a name derived from the channels in the sand molds which resembled a mother pig nursing piglets). At that point the iron maker could remelt the pig iron either to make cast iron or to be reworked further into wrought iron. Then wrought iron could be reheated again and passed through rollers or hammered into bars, sheets, or specific products.

The first iron blast furnaces in the Great Allegheny Passage region opened in the mountains of Fayette County in the 1790s. Many more small operations followed. Within a few decades, a handful of larger iron companies such as Maryland's Mount Savage Iron Works turned out both pig iron and iron goods. Chartered in 1837, the Mount Savage Iron Works operated two blast furnaces and a rolling mill that produced the nation's first iron railroad rails in 1844. In 1812, Pittsburgh's first steam-powered rolling mill was built. By 1842, rolling mills and

Exterior of Cold Blast Furnace. *Drawing by Clarence McWilliams for* The Planting of Civilization in Western Pennsylvania, *by Solon J. and Elizabeth Hawthorne Buck.*

foundries, using the pig iron of the rural blast furnaces, had so multiplied in Pittsburgh that a visiting Charles Dickens compared the city with Birmingham, England, observing: "It certainly has a great quantity of smoke hanging over it, and is famous for its iron works."

While the rural blast furnaces depended on charcoal and hence the timber of the surrounding forests, the steam-powered mills of Pittsburgh and western Maryland's Allegany County burned coal. Bituminous coal of considerable variation in quality is widely distributed across the Appalachian Plateau from Ohio to Alabama. Varying in thickness from five to fourteen feet, the Pittsburgh coal bed underlies much of southwestern Pennsylvania, western Maryland, and northern West Virginia. The outcroppings of coal at the surface in many areas and its frequent availability through shallow mines made coal mining relatively easy and inexpensive during the agrarian era. Where a coal seam was exposed on the surface, it was stripped by pick and shovel. Coal could also be uncovered by drift mining. A drift mine used a coal car pulled by a hoisting engine or carried up a slope by conveyor belts. Drift mines were dug upward at a slight angle to allow water to drain naturally from the mine. Coal was even mined for local industries from the hillside across from the Monongahela wharf in Pittsburgh, now Mount Washington, but once known as Coal Hill. Thus, wherever coal could be economically gathered and transported to the river or later canals, it found markets in the distant cities' industries and homes.

Frostburg, Maryland, on the Great Allegheny Passage Trail, became a center for coal shipment during the second quarter of the century because it was located amid the "Big Vein" of coalfields running from the Pennsylvania border southward for twenty-five miles through the Georges Creek Valley to the Potomac River. Relatively accessible coal and successful shipping down the Potomac River by flatboat and later along the C&O Canal attracted outside capital for mining well before midcentury. Mines operated at Lonaconing, Mount Savage, and several other small towns in the area. Large-scale mining west of the mountains, however, awaited the tremendous demands of rapid urban and industrial growth that came after 1850.

The transformation of the region after midcentury was accelerated by great improvements in moving bulk goods on the rivers and by rail. Increasing needs for natural resources spurred efforts to advance navigation on the Potomac, Monongahela, and Youghiogheny rivers. However, seasonal fluctuations in river flow, navigational hazards such as rapids and sandbars, and floods frequently impeded commerce. Attempts to remove snags and other obstacles, dynamite boulders and ripples, and dredge sandbars proved to be ineffective. Advocates turned to more expensive locks and dams to create slack-water navigation—a constant pool of water between the dams that retained a navigable depth—that could expand navigational seasons, extend the navigable extent of the rivers, and diminish the risks of commercial shipping. Incorporated in 1836 by an act of the Pennsylvania State Assembly, the Monongahela Navigation Company intended to erect a series of dams between Pittsburgh and the Virginia (now West Virginia) state line. The completion of Lock #4 in 1844 opened slack-water navigation between Pittsburgh and Brownsville.

Slack-water navigation to Brownsville, where the National Road crossed the Monongahela, fostered some interregional trade. Goods from the West headed eastward to Cumberland and Baltimore via the river and the National Road, while Baltimore merchants sent various kinds of saleable goods westward along these same routes, at least until the railroads eclipsed the river and road networks after the Civil War. The improved navigation stimulated development within the Great Allegheny Passage region. Merchandise shipped on the river included agricultural surplus, small numbers of livestock, and manufactured items such as flour, whiskey, bacon, lard, bricks, glass, and wood products (shingles, lath, staves, hoop-poles, posts, and boards). By far, however, extractive products such as coal, sand, salt, stone, and timber made up the bulk of the tonnage. In particular, the slack-water system allowed the coal trade from southwestern Pennsylvania to Pittsburgh to expand rapidly.

The Monongahela navigation scheme triggered efforts to create slack water on the Youghiogheny River in order to enhance the coal trade. The Youghiogheny flowed into the Monongahela River at McKeesport and was already navigable for about six miles from this confluence. The Youghiogheny Navigation Company was formed in 1843 to extend slack water by Boston and Buena Vista—both towns on the Great Allegheny Passage—18.5 miles upriver to West Newton. Locks were completed and navigation underway in 1850. But after a promising beginning, frequent damage to locks and dams by ice and floods on the swift-flowing Youghiogheny led to the company's insolvency by 1858 and the demise of navigation by the mid-1860s.

Pressure mounted on the federal government to solve western navigational problems. The Army Corps of Engineers eventually installed locks and dams in the upper Ohio watershed in the late nineteenth and early twentieth centuries, which guaranteed a navigable depth of nine feet in all seasons. After 1910, Congress provided authorization to deepen the entire Ohio system, including long portions of the Monongahela and Allegheny rivers, to that depth.

During the agrarian years, slow and cumbersome flatboats were a mainstay of the river routes. Large flatboats as long as eighty feet were built at Cumberland, loaded with coal and other regional products, and launched on the Potomac with the annual spring freshets, or high waters. West of the mountains, flatboats made the perilous journey down the Ohio, often as far as New Orleans. As trade on the region's rivers in western Maryland and southwestern Pennsylvania became an established way of life, the boat-building industry flourished. In Brownsville, Elizabeth, Pittsburgh, Cumberland, and a few other small river towns, builders fashioned all manner of vessels, from flatboats and keelboats to steamboats and barges, to handle the commerce, especially down the Ohio River

The flatboats' lack of speed, however, as well as one-way traffic downriver, limited the utility of these vessels. Steamboats solved the problem of transporting goods upriver. They dramatically increased the volume of goods moving along the western rivers, and, as a result, significantly reduced transport costs. In short, steamboats transformed western commerce. The first steamboat on western waters was built in Pittsburgh in 1811 and named the *New Orleans* for its planned

Men using a steam thresher to fill a granary in Somerset County. Courtesy Mary S. Biesecker Public Library.

destination. By the mid-1820s, steamboats regularly pulled into ports all along the Ohio River, and within a couple of decades improvements in technology and design allowed them to ply tributary rivers like the Allegheny and Monongahela. As navigation became progressively more dependable after 1850, steamboat traffic continued to expand, especially for the purpose of transporting coal. Along with the locks and dams, steam power turned the Monongahela into a river of industry, and coal dominated the river's traffic.

Steamboats were a harbinger of the industrialization that would transform life in the Great Allegheny Passage region. Entrepreneurs applied steam engines, powered with the region's coal, to many manufacturing enterprises. By the 1830s, Pittsburgh already stood out nationally as a center for steam engines' use and manufacture, but no application of that technology had a greater impact on the region than the steam railroad.

The steam railroad first reached the Great Allegheny Passage in the 1840s, and in the years after the Civil War fulfilled the dreams of those who had for more than a hundred years searched for an efficient means of crossing the mountains. Railroads became the way to travel. They were fast, powerful, and romantic. They tied the disparate parts of America together with steel rails. Railroads took people to new places, brought food to the table, transported iron and steel to markets where the future was being constructed, and carried men and military supplies to war.

The railroad era was full of ceaseless competition. The first lines competed with canals and soon replaced most of them. They competed with each other, buying or building short lines to haul freight to their main trunk lines. Railroad entrepreneurs, adept at financing and takeovers, concocted systems that linked routes covering unimaginable distances. In the Great Allegheny Passage region, a vast network of mainline and short-haul railroads crisscrossed the coalfields and rivers during the industrial era, becoming a familiar part of the countryside.

The cheapest railway construction in the region of the Great Allegheny Passage was along riverbanks, where nature itself had removed obstacles to laying down track. The ancient drainage basins of rivers in the Allegheny Mountains and Plateau were full of valleys with narrow floodplains of sand and gravel left behind by thousands of years of erosion and deposition by the westward-flowing rivers, from the Casselman to the Youghiogheny, then to the Monongahela and the Ohio. Tracks had to be laid high enough along the banks to avoid regular floods, and viaducts, bridges, and tunnels were required; but the main routes of developing railroad networks were never in doubt.

In 1827, the state of Maryland granted a charter to investors for constructing a railroad to the Ohio River. Fifteen years later this pioneering railroad, the B&O, reached Cumberland. Unable to receive a

charter from the state of Pennsylvania, which protected the interests of
Philadelphia and the westward-expanding Pennsylvania Railroad, the
B&O could not reach Pittsburgh, and instead constructed track to the
Ohio River at Wheeling. The first B&O train reached Wheeling in 1853,
about the same time the Pennsylvania Railroad entered Pittsburgh.

Coal inspired the development of short-line railroads within the
region. In 1845, for example, a railroad went from Cumberland through
the Narrows and on to Mount Savage. It was extended south to Frostburg in 1851 and six years later to Lonaconing. Another ran from Cumberland to Eckhart. By 1864, the Cumberland and Pennsylvania Rail-

B&O Railroad at Ferncliff Park, Ohiopyle, about 1890.

road, owned by the Consolidated Coal Company, controlled these lines in one system through the Maryland coalfields.

West of the mountains, the Pittsburgh and Connellsville Railroad began operations in 1855 along the Youghiogheny from Connellsville to West Newton, which was considered the head of navigation when the locks and dams on the river were still operating. In 1860, the Pittsburgh and Connellsville connected to Pittsburgh, and eleven years later it extended east from Connellsville to Cumberland. In 1875, it was taken over by the ambitious B&O, which had finally been granted a charter four years earlier by the state of Pennsylvania to extend into Pittsburgh.

During the "Railroad Wars" of the last part of the nineteenth century, Andrew Carnegie and William H. Vanderbilt tried to construct new lines across Pennsylvania, under the auspices of the ephemeral South Pennsylvania Railroad, to break the lock that the Pennsylvania Railroad had on the coal, coke, and steel trades. One consequence of this competition was the creation of another short-lived railroad, the Pittsburgh, McKeesport, and Youghiogheny (called the P-Mickey) in 1883. Funded by Vanderbilt to extend his future (but unbuilt) South Pennsylvania Railroad into Pittsburgh, the track was completed to Connellsville and then leased to the Pittsburgh and Lake Erie (P&LE) Railroad.

The P&LE served the coalfields, iron mills, and steelworks of the Pittsburgh industrial region. It was called the "Little Giant" for the lucrative earnings it generated per ton/mile along its comparatively short, double-tracked route. Formed in 1875, the P&LE built its track through the industrializing Beaver and Mahoning river valleys north of Pittsburgh to Youngstown, Ohio. With its lease of the P-Mickey in 1884 and the construction of a branch to Brownsville, it connected the Connellsville coke district to the blast furnaces and steel mills of the Monongahela Valley as well as along its original route. Its line from Pittsburgh to Connellsville on the southern bank of the Youghiogheny River, opposite the B&O, constitutes a key segment of the Great Allegheny Passage trail. The Youghiogheny branch had stops at places that today's bikers along the Passage recognize, such as Boston, Dravo, Buena Vista, West Newton, and Cedar Creek. The P&LE built a magnificent station in Pittsburgh, which exists today as Station Square, a trailhead in Pittsburgh.

The volume of commerce east of Connellsville toward Baltimore eventually supported a rival to the B&O, the Western Maryland (WM)

Railway. The Western Maryland originated in the Civil War era, and by 1872 operated a line from Baltimore to Hagerstown, Maryland. The railroad extended to Cumberland in 1906, where it connected with the West Virginia Central, which carried timber and coal northward from its namesake state. Nonetheless, the WM slipped into financial and legal difficulties in 1908 and was placed under the auspices of a court-appointed administrator. With new investment from J. D. Rockefeller, the WM built a line to Connellsville in 1912, four decades after the B&O steamed into that city, and found renewed life in the access to the coal and coke trade. Called "the fast freight line" and the "Wild Mary" because of its speed, the WM hauled coal and freight for sixty years. Its fine railroad station at Meyersdale is a stopping point on today's Great Allegheny Passage, and other station houses were located at Garrett, Rockwood, Confluence, and Ohiopyle. By the 1970s, the declining coal trade drove the WM out of business; it was absorbed by the rival B&O.

Twentieth-century engineering and construction techniques had allowed the WM to tunnel through mountains and cross valleys on viaducts and bridges that were impossible to build when the B&O had first laid down its tracks on a more easily engineered path a generation earlier. The landmark structures of the WM provide memorable experiences on the Great Allegheny Passage. These include the Brush, Borden, and Pinkerton tunnels. The largest, Big Savage Tunnel, was a modern engineering marvel when it was constructed. So too was the Salisbury Viaduct, which had to span the Casselman River and the two-track mainline of the B&O. A new electric crane moved the viaduct's giant steel girders into place, but on July 10, 1911, the crane toppled to the valley floor ninety-five feet below, killing six men and injuring another. Another worker fell to his death a month after.

One more former railroad route contributes to the Great Allegheny Passage biking experience. The Montour Railroad was a short-haul line typical of the coalfields during the expansive years of industrial railroading. It was built in 1877 to collect coal from local mines west and south of Pittsburgh and deliver it to towns such as Coraopolis on the Ohio River. The Montour eventually extended to the Monongahela River, a few miles south of McKeesport. It once served as many as thirty local mines, but it closed in the 1970s because of the depletion of coal resources. Because it connects the Monongahela to the Ohio River in its semicircular route west and south of Pittsburgh, the path of the former Montour Railroad provides an alternative to biking into the city along the Great Allegheny Passage trail.

The region's vast bituminous coal resources and in particular the superior coal for making coke of the Connellsville district were fundamental to the region's industrial transformation, especially for metropolitan Pittsburgh's preeminent iron and steel industry. The arrival of the railroads, which both carried and consumed coal, as well as the growth of industry and cities drew capital investment to develop mines throughout the region of the Great Allegheny Passage. With significant corporate investment already in place before 1870, a relatively small area of western Maryland steadily produced coal during the late nineteenth century—4.5 million tons in 1901 alone. Intensive coal production in the eight southwestern Pennsylvania counties started later, but soon dwarfed Maryland's output. Total production of nine million tons in 1881 expanded to nearly fifty million tons in 1901 and eighty-two million tons forty years later. Drift and slope mines (the latter angled downhill to reach the vein, requiring both hoisting machinery and water pumps) predominated into the early twentieth century, but more costly shaft mining, which involved driving a deep, vertical shaft down to the vein, requiring much greater investment, became increasingly common. Much of the region's coal was best suited to produce steam for railroads and industry, but shortly after the Civil War the portion of the Pittsburgh coal bed known as the Connellsville coal seam, located in both Fayette and Westmoreland counties, was recognized as ideal, physically and chemically, for producing beehive coke. With new coking technology adopted after 1900, coal available west and north of the Connellsville district in Fayette, Washington, and Greene counties became prized for coke too.

Coke is essentially bituminous coal baked under controlled temperatures to burn off the chemical impurities, leaving behind hard nuggets of largely carbon—an ideal fuel for iron and steel furnaces. Connellsville coke was surprisingly pure, porous, and hard enough to withstand transportation without breaking down. The plants were located at the coal mines to reduce transportation costs, since enormous amounts of coal were required for the process. Coking reduced a ton (2,000 pounds) of coal to about 1,200 to 1,300 pounds of coke.

Until the adoption of the by-product coking process in the early twentieth century, beehive ovens in the Connellsville district were the main source of coke for the Pittsburgh iron and steel industry. Named for their interior domed shape, beehive ovens were charged with coal dumped from wagons or lorry cars at the top of a line of ovens. Workers leveled the coal inside for an even burn; then bricked up the oven door and burned the coal for forty-eight hours for furnace coke or seventy-two hours for foundry coke. At the end of that time, they removed the bricks from the door and sprayed water on the coke to cool it down. Finally, workers raked the coke directly into railroad cars or into wheelbarrows for carting to the cars. Beehive ovens were either built into hillsides or in freestanding parallel rows or blocks. A coke plant could contain as few as 50 ovens or more than 500. The Standard Coke Works in Mount Pleasant, Pennsylvania, had 905 ovens.

The coal seam defining the superior coking coal of the Connellsville district trended for about fifty miles along a southwest to northeast axis in front of Chestnut Ridge, Pennsylvania. Only about six miles wide, the district stretched from Latrobe in Westmoreland County southwest past Uniontown in Fayette County toward the Monongahela River and the West Virginia border. Connellsville, located on the Youghiogheny River, was at its center. Coal mines, coke plants, railroads, and adjacent company towns constituted the typical coke complex. During the peak years of production, about one hundred coke plants were spread about the district.

Despite rising demand by furnace operators in Pittsburgh, coke production grew slowly during the 1860s. The first real boom occurred in the 1870s, but it was dampened somewhat by the severe economic depression during the middle of the decade. After 1880, the beehive coke industry took off. The 7,200 ovens in the Connellsville area in 1880 leaped to 16,000 in 1890 and 39,000 by 1910. During these years, the region averaged 50 percent or more of the nation's coke production, and had truly become a "Cloud by Day," a phrase used by author Muriel Sheppard to title her book about the industry.

New technologies, especially by-product ovens, facilitated the use of poorer coals to be used for coke and, thus, the spread of the industry in the region and into other states. After 1900, for example, coal operators rushed to open mines and coke plants west and northwest of Connellsville in the Lower Connellsville District, or "Klondike" area, between the Youghiogheny and Monongahela rivers. The efficient by-product ovens captured the coal gases produced during coking and used them to heat blast furnaces, open hearth furnaces, power stations, and

Remains of the Allison ovens, 1982. Courtesy Eugene Levy.

other plants. Coal was transported to by-product plants near the iron and steel mills, where the gases could be efficiently used. The great steel companies, such as Jones and Laughlin, built their own coke plants. U.S. Steel's giant coke-making facility in Clairton, Pennsylvania, erected in 1918 along the Monongahela a few miles upriver from its junction with the Youghiogheny, still operates today. By-product coke spelled the end of the less efficient beehive plants, and the older Connellsville district's coal resources were being rapidly depleted. By-product coke production surpassed Connellsville coke by 1920; the Great Depression sounded the final toll for Connellsville's coke industry.

Fortunes were made and lost in the coke business. In the fertile valley just south of Perryopolis, for example, the Cochran family of Dawson, Pennsylvania (notably father James and son Philip), installed the Washington Coal and Coke Company in the town of Star Junction, near the Passage. Established in the 1890s, this coke works housed nearly one thousand ovens, and altered forever the economic and social structure of the rural area where George Washington had once built his grist mill. Philip Cochran's wife, Sarah, built a magnificent mansion called Linden Hall in Dawson, which still stands today.

Another giant of the industry was Uniontown's J. V. K. Thompson, who built and lost his fortune speculating in the coal resources of Lower Connellsville and the lands across the Monongahela River in Greene County. The extravagant behavior and consumption of his much younger, second wife—Honey Hawes—titillated and scandalized the locals even though she spent most of her time in New York and Paris. The no-nonsense Presbyterian J. V. evinced the area's work ethic, but Honey was always exotic to the region.

The dominant force in the Connellsville coke industry was Henry Clay Frick. He grew up on a hardscrabble farm near Mount Pleasant, but set out to be as rich as his maternal grandfather Abraham Overholt, the whiskey manufacturer for whom he had worked as a young man. Frick saw that steel-making was to become a principal industry and focused his early business career on supplying coke to it. In 1871, he began leasing and buying all the coal lands that he could accumulate in the Connellsville region, and then building coke ovens on them At the age of twenty-one, Frick approached the formidable Pittsburgh investment banker Judge Thomas Mellon for a $10,000 loan to build fifty ovens at Broad Ford on the Youghiogheny River. He got the loan and, despite a depression, soon returned to Judge Mellon for another $10,000 to build even more ovens. Frick reinvested aggressively in more coking lands and ovens during the 1870s. By 1880 he controlled one thousand coke ovens and three thousand acres of land. Frick was a millionaire by the time he was thirty, and moved to Pittsburgh where he could expand his business horizons.

During his honeymoon in 1881, Frick and his wife, Adelaide,

dined with Andrew Carnegie, already a customer of Frick's coke. By the end of that meal, Frick had agreed to reorganize his coke company in a partnership with the steelmaker. By 1894, H. C. Frick Coal and Coke Company operated 7,100 ovens, which constituted 40 percent of the district's capacity. Carnegie liked the laconic Frick's direct, ruthless management style and saw in him the executive officer for his steel company that he needed while he himself set policy and sold products from his residences in New York and Scotland. Frick vertically integrated Carnegie Steel, making it the nation's largest steel firm in the 1890s. These two ambitious, strong-willed, but quite different personalities engaged in a twenty-year, tempestuous partnership that became legendary for its business success and public rancor.

Pittsburgh transformed from the Iron City in the 1850s into the Steel City of popular legend by the 1890s. When novelist Theodore Dreiser arrived at the P&LE station in Pittsburgh in the 1890s and walked out onto Smithfield Street, the symbolic nature of Pittsburgh was forced upon him, as it had been on countless other visitors before him: "The whole river for a mile or more was suddenly lit with a rosy glow, a glow which, I saw upon turning, came from the tops of some forty or fifty stacks belching an orange-red flame. At the same time an enormous pounding and cracking came from somewhere, as though titans were at work upon subterranean anvils."

Close to him on the city's South Side was the Oliver Iron and Steel Company, and beyond that the Jones and Laughlin American Iron Works, two giant mills that fronted the Monongahela near downtown Pittsburgh. Had Dreiser gone further up the Monongahela, he would have passed the Carnegie mills at Braddock, Homestead, and Duquesne, and then reached McKeesport with its massive steel- and pipe-making operations. More mills would soon arise farther up the river.

A half century earlier, Pittsburgh's already sizable iron industry flourished with forges, foundries, and rolling mills. But in the 1850s and 1860s, burgeoning demand for iron by the rapidly expanding railroads, the Civil War, and urban-industrial growth itself challenged the city's ironmasters to expand production. Expansion required new sources of pig iron, for the traditional country blast furnaces could not provide enough to meet the mills' increasing appetite. The recognition of the superior quality of coke from the Connellsville district encouraged the development of blast furnaces in Pittsburgh. Beginning with the first furnace in 1859, Pittsburgh producers created over the years an aggressive and innovative blast furnace industry that produced more than a quarter of the nation's pig iron by the end of the century.

When Andrew Carnegie started investing in iron manufacturing in the 1860s, the industry used the old style of manufacture in which each stage from raw materials to finished products took place in separate, independent units. Blast furnaces smelted the ore into pig iron; forges, puddling furnaces and rolling mills converted pig iron into bars and slabs; other mills then rolled rails, plates, sheets, and cut nails. Separate foundries and factories fabricated tools, hardware, pots and pans, stoves, and other items. A small partnership or proprietorship would own one or more of these production units.

In the 1850s iron railroad rails presented especially attractive market opportunities, and for a few decades mills were expanded to meet the demand. However, in the 1860s, several ironmasters around the nation attempted to mass produce steel for rails as a means to capture this lucrative market. At the time, steel was a highly specialized and expensive metal made in small quantities until the new Bessemer technology was devised to mass produce it from the traditional iron-making process. Iron products were comparatively brittle or soft. Steel on the other hand is an alloy of pure iron to which carbon has been added to increase its strength. The Bessemer process was a breakthrough in making steel. It converted pig iron into steel by sending blasts of air through molten iron, removing impurities and producing a superior metal in large quantities.

Andrew Carnegie decided to try his hand at the emerging and lucrative business of producing steel rails. In 1875, he built the large Edgar Thomson works in Braddock, Pennsylvania, on the Monongahela River. Twelve miles upstream from Pittsburgh, Edgar Thomson was the most modern mill of its kind at the time and was enormously successful from the start. Carnegie designed it to use the latest steel-making technology and ran it with groundbreaking management strategies, such as insisting on accurate cost estimates and keeping track of what every department was doing in the process. This system of detailed costs per unit of output for materials and labor gave management unprecedented control over decision making. The culmination of Carnegie's innovative thinking was vertical integration that combined once-separate processes, eliminated middlemen, coordinated operations, minimized inventories, eliminated duplication of machinery, and shifted skilled workers to address temporary needs. Carnegie bought his competition, mills at the nearby Monongahela River towns of Homestead and Duquesne, to form the largest steel company in the nation. As the president of Carnegie's steel company, Frick coordinated production among the mills, bought iron ore deposits in the upper Great Lakes area, and ran a steamship line and railroads for smooth transport between various facilities. Carnegie Steel became the core of the newly created U.S. Steel in 1901, making Carnegie "the richest man in the world." Carnegie spent the rest of his life as a philanthropist.

Other regional producers soon followed Carnegie's example, erect-

View at Braddocks Fields, At the Edgar Thomson Steel Works. *Lithograph, 1876.*

ing Bessemer works and later adding open hearth steel-making furnaces, which progressively replaced Bessemer production. In 1874, Pittsburgh had thirty-eight iron and steel mills, mostly turning out iron goods and only 8.7 percent of the nation's steel. By the turn of the century, there were sixty-three mills in the Pittsburgh district that produced nearly 40 percent of American crude steel. The traveler on the Great Allegheny Passage today passes through the former sites of historic mills of Carnegie Steel, Jones and Laughlin, and Oliver Iron and Steel, among others, now mostly redeveloped for a variety of commercial and residential uses. Across the river from the trail, the furnaces of the active Edgar Thomson works of U.S. Steel, modernized once more in the 1990s to remain competitive, rise above the vegetation of the river bank to remind one of the early industrial era. Just downstream from Braddock, two of the remaining, though inactive, blast furnaces of U.S Steel's Carrie Furnaces loom over the river, designated a national historic landmark in 2006. In Pittsburgh, the Hot Metal Bridge, which once carried Jones and Laughlin's hoppers of molten iron from their blast furnaces in Hazelwood across the Monongahela River for conversion to steel and processing in the company's South Side works, now carries cars, as well as bikers traversing the Great Allegheny Passage.

Epitomized by the huge integrated mills of the Monongahela Valley, the Pittsburgh metropolitan industrial area was a vast complex of mines, mills, and factories. Besides the integrated mills, the iron and steel industry included many independent iron blast furnace operators; metal fabricators such as bridge companies; bar, sheet, and tin plate works; pipe, tube, wire, and nail mills; and a host of machinery makers and machine shops. In addition to the steel industry, a variety of corporations made Pittsburgh one of the largest metropolitan areas in 1920. Henry John Heinz erected his giant food processing plant on the city's North Side. George Westinghouse built his great electric equipment factory and his air-brake plant along Turtle Creek near Braddock, just a few miles from the Monongahela, and his railroad signaling works in nearby Swissvale. George Mesta built the giant, mile-long Mesta Machine Company in West Homestead, becoming the world's leading manufacturer of steel-making equipment. The Aluminum Company of America (ALCOA) and Pittsburgh Plate Glass (PPG Industries) erected large plants along the Allegheny River, and other glass, mining machinery, and railroad equipment companies existed in many towns that constituted Pittsburgh's metropolitan area.

At the terminus of the Great Allegheny Passage in downtown Pittsburgh, the skyscrapers remind travelers of the enormous capital concentrated in the city's banks, investment houses, and corporate headquarters. The cluster of banks along two blocks of Fourth Avenue was known as Pittsburgh's Wall Street. Investment bankers Judge Thomas Mellon and his sons Andrew W. and Richard B. Mellon amassed fortunes no less spectacular than those of Carnegie and Frick.

Jones and Laughlin Steel Corporation, Soho Works, 1931. Courtesy Carnegie Museum of Art.

For a century, Pittsburgh as much as any city symbolized American manufacturing, reaching new heights of production during World War II. Nonetheless, the Pittsburgh area's achievements must not obscure those of Cumberland and its Maryland hinterland. At the other end of the Great Allegheny Passage, Cumberland benefited from its location at the nexus of several important transportation routes and proximity to coal, pig iron, and timber. In addition to the National Road, Cumberland shipped goods eastward along the C&O Canal and especially enjoyed the access afforded by the B&O Railroad to the mid-Atlantic markets and to the Midwest via the Ohio Valley and Pittsburgh. A steel rail and bar mill opened in 1870 and operated successfully into the 1880s. Foundries produced agricultural and mining equipment as well as various other iron goods, and a tin plate mill went into service in 1892. The B&O operated repair shops and a rail yard. With access to the region's forest, the small city had sawmills, a sash and furniture factory, carriage works, and tanneries. Like Pittsburgh, Cumberland also had glassworks. After World War I, the Kelly-Springfield Tire Company and the Celanese Corporation, a producer of synthetic fibers, both erected large plants. Elsewhere in western Maryland and particularly in Frostburg, companies manufactured mining equipment, small locomotives, firebricks, and lumber products. The railroads employed many workers in repair shops, stations, and yards, as well.

If the Great Allegheny Passage reminds one of the sometimes spectacular entrepreneurship legendary in America's story of its industrialization, it even more poignantly reveals the hard work, craftsmanship, pride, sacrifice, and sometimes violent struggle of the men, women, and children who worked in the mines, mills, factories, logging camps, and railroad yards. In the nineteenth century, immigrants flocked to the region for work. Skilled miners and metal workers, along

Coke workers at Henry C. Frick's South West Coal and Coke Oven #3, north of Scottdale, purchased by Frick in 1885.

with their unskilled brethren, came from the British Isles; others left their homes in Ireland and Germany. Unskilled immigrants from southern and eastern Europe followed them after the 1880s, while a much smaller steady stream of African Americans filtered in from America's southeastern states.

In the Steel Valley, the story of steelworker Joe Magarac came, via Hungarian legend, to symbolize the laborer who was made of steel himself. The myth has Magarac born in a mountain of iron ore, and portrays him as a Slavic giant, capable of bending steel bars with his bare hands. He wins a beautiful bride in a contest of strength, but refuses to wed because it will interfere with his work. Finally, he leaps into a Bessemer converter and becomes part of the steel being made for a new mill, which will in turn make more steel. The myth expresses the

Joe Magarac, legendary Man of Steel.

pride people had in their work; but it may also have been a means to cope with the notoriously difficult conditions under which they labored and lived.

Work in the mines and mills was physically punishing; the hours were long, conditions dangerous, employment insecure, and wages inadequate. The heat, light, noise, and danger of steelmaking epitomized the epic character of nation's heavy industry. Coal mining was less dramatic, but no less exhausting or dangerous. The men came out of the mines covered in black coal dust; if there was a bathhouse, they, like the steel workers, used its shower, putting their work clothes in baskets hanging overhead. Otherwise, they cleaned up as well as possible at home, where running water was not always available. Workers toiled in a din of whistles, steam engines, hammering, and any number of operating machines. The most dreaded noise, however, was an unscheduled loud whistle signaling a work-related disaster. In a mine, a roof would collapse, an explosion would occur because of collected gas, or an underground flood would drive out the air. When a rat decided to leave, the men followed. Rats lived close to the miners, sometimes ate their food, and served as scavengers of waste left in the mine. A rat's keen hearing, plus its position closer to the coal and ground, was believed to detect the early signs of the earth "working" or possibly a cave-in. Rats also avoided methane gas and black damp, an atmosphere deficient in oxygen usually because of too much carbon dioxide.

Outside the workplace, housing was often overcrowded, flimsy, poorly insulated (if at all), and unsanitary. Adjacent to the mills and mines, neighborhoods were noisy, dirty, and dense. Employers, especially in mining company or "patch" towns, often exercised absolute power over workers' lives and municipal officials. Indeed, social reformers surveyed Pittsburgh in 1907 and 1908 in order to depict for the nation an archetypal example of industrial capitalism's evils.

The inevitable consequence of hard-driving capitalists like Carnegie and Frick and the proud workers, who had a work ethic second to none, was a history studded with labor disputes over wages, hours, working conditions, and trade union recognition. Increasingly intolerable working conditions and the diminution of skilled workers' roles accompanied industrialization during the second half of the nineteenth century. Many workers saw this trend as the metamorphosis of "free

Tenements at Valley works, near Scottdale, c. 1893.

labor" into "wage slavery." Workers organized in trade unions, and labor protests and work stoppages broke out frequently throughout the region. A few strikes took on national significance. In 1877, railroad workers in several cities across the nation, including Cumberland and Pittsburgh, protested a cut in wages during the severe depression and within the context of a history of the railroad's abuse of power. Railroad men and sympathetic workers from other unions impeded the progress of trains. In Pittsburgh, a militia from Philadelphia brought in to quell the strike ignited devastating violence. The Pennsylvania Railroad's large depot was burned to the ground, hundreds of locomotives and railroad cars were looted and destroyed, at least twenty-four people were killed, and many more injured. The damages were estimated in the millions. The conclusion of the strike hardened attitudes on both sides of labor issues.

Wage cuts in the region's mines triggered frequent strikes, often mercilessly put down to the hardship of miners and their families. At the same time, increasing mass production in the mills weakened the hand of once-powerful skilled workers, who through their unions sought to retain their status. The Amalgamated Association of Iron and Steel Workers fought a last stand in Homestead in 1892 against Carnegie and Frick, men determined to defeat the union once and for all regardless of the specific issues under contention. Andrew Carnegie, on his annual vacation in Scotland, gave authority to win the strike by whatever means necessary to Frick, who was already well known for his ruthless treatment of labor in the coke district. Frick erected a wooden fence around the mill to keep strikers out. To secure the mill and protect non-union workers, he hired three hundred armed Pinkerton guards to move secretly upstream at night on two barges from ten miles downriver of Pittsburgh. The workers were alerted and prepared to defend their jobs. When the Pinkertons arrived, a gunfight ensued; workers used dynamite, cannon, and burning oil to try to destroy the barges. The Pinkertons could not land, and at length surrendered. When they left the barges, they had to walk a gauntlet among enraged workers and their families, who beat them before imprisoning them in a building. Ten strikers and three Pinkertons were killed, and many others wounded.

"Homestead Troubles." *Cover of* Frank Leslie's Illustrated, *July 14, 1892.*

At Frick's request, the governor of Pennsylvania called out the National Guard to occupy the town, protect the mill, and arrest the strike leaders. Sympathy strikes broke out in other steel mills, and Congress debated the uses of private police to break the unions. A little more than two weeks after the strike began, a young revolutionary anarchist named Alexander Berkman tried to assassinate Frick in his office in downtown Pittsburgh. Frick was wounded and the assassin captured, but Frick gained a measure of popular sympathy. The strike ended in a defeat for the union. Carnegie and Frick put the best possible face on the bloody battle at Homestead; but when Carnegie expressed regret at the treatment of the strikers, relations between the two industrialists worsened and were never recovered.

The battle of Homestead illuminated the serious divisions between labor and industry—economic, social, political, and ethical problems—that remained unaddressed for many years. Unions in western Pennsylvania and the steel industry had been dealt a blow that lasted for decades, and the poor conditions in which steelworkers continued to labor became part of a national debate about exploitation. Meanwhile, the flood of immigrants from eastern and southern Europe kept the labor supply both abundant and cheap, while technological progress and mechanical efficiencies eliminated some jobs in the mills and mines. Differences in language and religion among the workers, combined with traditional ethnic and national rivalries, divided the workforce. Company power in the mills and the industrial communities further inhibited successful union representation and strategies. Although strikes continued in the mills and mines into the 1930s, only the passage of federal legislation in 1936 during the New Deal gave workers the legal footing necessary to organize successfully, strike effectively, and improve working conditions and the lives of their families.

After 1920, the entire Great Allegheny Passage region experienced a decline in industrial growth. The expansion phase of coal mining, metals manufacturing, and lumbering had come to an end. These industries now had to compete within the changing national context of new markets, emerging technologies, and even declining natural resources. Moreover, the Great Depression was too severe and long for many companies to survive. Others recovered during World War II, but afterward still faced the pressures of a changing economy. Many mines and logging operations closed; oil and gas industries challenged the importance of coal; steel companies erected mills closer to western markets or new sources of iron ore; railroads underwent a long-term decline as motor vehicles rapidly gained popularity; and glassmakers lost market share to plastic manufacturers. As mines, mills, and factories shuttered their plants, supporting equipment manufacturers and local service businesses declined and often closed as well. Brownfield sites in Cumberland, Connellsville, and other small industrial towns,

The Great Battle of Homestead. *Lithograph by Edwin Rowe, 1892.*

and most dramatically in the formerly mighty Monongahela Valley, replaced the once-vibrant industries familiar to the Great Allegheny Passage region. Many workers and their families moved away in search of jobs; others stayed. Overall, population declined. This transformation, which provided the opportunity for the bike trail, was unfathomable to those who knew the industrial era.

Along the Great Allegheny Passage, American industrial development from the pastoral eighteenth century through the twentieth century has left behind a long trail rich in signs and symbols for the observant traveler. Not only can one find the fascinating artifacts of canals and river dams, coal mines, railroads, bridges, tunnels, and mills, but also a legacy of people and their cultures, in small communities as well as in the postindustrial cities of the twenty-first century.

(left) The Great Allegheny Passage in Ohiopyle State Park.

Rock ledges of Loyalhanna Limestone between Ohiopyle and Confluence.

Unused Western Maryland Railway Bridge over the Youghiogheny River at Confluence.

Boaters at the confluence of the Youghiogheny and Casselman rivers.

Winter at the confluence of the Youghiogheny and Casselman rivers.

(right) Unnamed tributary stream along the trail.

Cyclists on the Passage alongside the Western Maryland Scenic Railroad.

THE SPIRIT OF THE PASSAGE

Where Past and Future Meet

KEVIN J. PATRICK

*T*he Great Allegheny Passage traverses a territory alive with tourists and tourist attractions, which share the stage with ghosts of the past and the remnant bits of historic landscape that have survived to recall a time when things were different. Youghiogheny touchstones bear witness to the opening skirmishes of the Seven Years' War, the canals and railroads that conquered the Alleghenies, the timber and coal used to trade natural beauty for jobs and development, and the ever-present tourists who first rode the rails to this mountain paradise and now come by the carload to create a new reality tied to recreation, conservation, and historic preservation.

Echoes from the past haunt the hollows of Jumonville: a moccasin footfall on a bed of leaves, the click of a brass button against a wooden musket stock. Barely audible in the moments before the ambush that would inflame two continents, these sounds are now a distant echo that has diminished to mere palpable sensation. The thunderclap of gunfire, shouts, and terror that followed on that May day in 1754 is lost, spent at the instant of discharge and impossible to call back. The stillness just before the clash that changed the fate of worlds clings yet to the rocky keep encircling the rim of Jumonville Glen, and holds in the air of the mountainside ensnared by the branches of growing trees not yet born at the time the warriors fell. Tourists who wander the carefully laid paths through the early morning serenity of Jumonville can still sense the moment of silence right before Major George Washington's two companies pounced on the unsuspecting and ill-fated French reconnaissance party touching off the Seven Years' War for North America.

Back over Chestnut Ridge to the east, inaudible echoes from the second stanza of this saga of continental conquest mingle with the ceaseless hum of traffic on Route 40. A momentarily victorious Washington fell back and hastily constructed Fort Necessity in preparation for the inevitable French retaliation, which arrived at one thousand strong, forcing Washington's surrender and solidifying the French hold over the critical Forks of the Ohio. Behind the whine of minivan tires bearing tourists to the Laurel Highlands are the ghosts of Major General Edward Braddock's demoralized army limping back across the mountains from his tragic advance on the French Fort Duquesne in July 1755. Braddock himself was ignominiously buried in the road to hide all traces of the body from possible desecration by victorious Indians, assumed to be in pursuit.

The sweat and blood and sinew of the retreating British soldiers penetrated the earth along the line of march and mixed with the moisture that rolled down from the drainage divide to be lost in the babbling waters of Meadow Run crashing and careening from rock to rock. Farther downstream and far into the future, catcalls and joyous laughter rise from kids riding the cascading froth of Meadow Run through "the slides" at Ohiopyle. Today's adventurous souls slip into the stream at the head of a steep, bare rock slope through which the interminable might of Meadow Run has entrenched a canted channel of fast-moving white-water that whisks brave thrill seekers bumping down a liquid chute of semi-controlled drowning. A short distance below, a quieter Meadow Run slips over a final ledge and into the boulder-strewn expanse of the Youghiogheny River. Immediately upstream from the mouth of Meadow Run, the Youghiogheny, more commonly known as just the Yough, is transformed into a shimmering curtain of falling white where the river plunges twenty feet over a precipice marking the Falls of Ohiopyle. Visitors rush to the rail of the overlook, as much elated with the view of the Falls as Washington was deflated with the realization that it rendered the Yough useless as a watery concourse for trans-Appalachian trade between the settled Atlantic seaboard and the fertile promise of the Ohio Valley. Where Washington saw not a single boat, thousands now pass every year loaded to the gunwales with vacationers going nowhere in vessels destined to run the same ten or twenty miles of river for their entire useful lives. The trade is in tourism, as whitewater rafting draws people *into* the mountains rather than through them.

Higher up the drainage basin at Grantsville, Maryland, a great stone arch vaults over the Casselman River, chief tributary to the upper Youghiogheny. Constructed in the remote Alleghenies in 1813 as the largest masonry arch on the continent, it is a monument to nation builders who disagreed with Washington's assessment of the Yough's potential as a navigable waterway. The high arch was built with high hopes to allow canal boats navigating a channelized Casselman unimpeded passage beneath the steady flow of traffic on the National Road. The trans-Appalachian waterway to the Ohio River was constructed as the Chesapeake and Ohio (C&O) Canal following the banks of the Potomac River west from Washington DC, but it never reached beyond

Bridge over the Casselman River at Little Crossings, Garrett County, Maryland. Photo by A. S. Burns, December 1933. Courtesy Historic American Buildings Survey, Library of Congress.

Cumberland, Maryland. It stalled here at the eastern foot of the Alleghenies in 1850, leaving the Casselman River un-channelized and free-flowing to the present day. The Casselman Bridge is now a historic artifact, a treasured jewel from the past set in its own landscaped park, overbuilt for the stream it crosses, but quaint in comparison to the twin spans of Interstate 68 passing within earshot. Bicycles now glide along the C&O towpath.

In Pennsylvania, the storied migrant road and its surviving bridges, taverns, and tollhouses have been reinterpreted as part of the National Road Heritage Corridor. The distinctive iron obelisks that marked the route for countless stagecoaches, freight wagons, and drovers' flocks have been joined by a multitude of replica markers to guide modern heritage tourists. Appearing freshly cast and painted, the retro-markers are actually made of Carsonite, a durable, lightweight, and inexpensive material with the ability to instantly shatter and break away when struck by wayward automobiles.

Deep within the Yough-carved recesses of the Allegheny Mountains, the river splashes through steep-sided gorges cloaked in dense forest. The Yough's watery blade has sliced a narrow path through the massive bulk of Laurel Ridge and Chestnut Ridge, two parallel mountains that rise from the intricately incised surface of the Allegheny Plateau. Despite the low-grade route provided by the river, its tortuous, steep-sided valley has, for most of its existence, been virtually impenetrable due to the rocky slopes that pitch down to the water's edge. Yet rising above the persistent whitewater noise of the river comes the occasional moan and mumbling rumble of artifice. The echoes of CSX trains that reverberate off the canyon walls are not shadows of the past but the modern successors of the mechanical beast that in 1871 breeched the Appalachian barrier through the natural course laid by the Youghiogheny River. Where one railroad sends its trains through the gorges of the Yough, there were once two. After 1912, coal drags, fast freights, and passenger trains of the Western Maryland (WM) Railroad powered through the gorges on the opposite bank. The trackless route is now laden with skid-lidded bicyclists who power themselves along a chipped stone path maintained as part of the Great Allegheny Passage.

The Great Allegheny Passage is the latest attempt to use the Youghiogheny River Valley to conquer the Appalachian barrier, this time with a 150-mile recreational bike path connecting Pittsburgh and Cumberland over the route of the abandoned Pittsburgh and Lake Erie (P&LE) Railroad and Western Maryland Railway. The bike path is a significant piece of infrastructure aiding the transformation of the Youghiogheny River Valley from remote, industrial fringe to the primary tourist destination of southwestern Pennsylvania. It is the product of an attitude change about the region's environment, away from its previous exploitation as a resource and toward its current conservation as a natural habitat and historic landscape. Through recent conservation and historic preservation initiatives, leisure travelers striking out on the Great Allegheny Passage experience the scenic majesty of the mountains while coming to appreciate the Herculean effort expended to conquer, live on, exploit, and finally, live *with* the Alleghenies.

The Youghiogheny landscape that the tourist experiences has been assembled through the ages. Like autumn leaves accumulating on the forest floor at the end of each season, the detritus of one historical period covers the last, though not entirely. Gradually decaying away beneath the new layer, bits and pieces of the previous periods readily show through and are even incorporated into the maturing landscape of any given time. Just when some stasis appears to have been reached that allows an observer to declare, *this* is the Youghiogheny, another season of change comes about and carpets the landscape with a fresh look.

The earliest layer of human habitation lies light on the modern Yough Valley, imparting both scattered bits of trash left behind by a "Monongahela" people so long lost that we do not even know their real name and such intangibles as place names and stories of young George Washington and the tragic defeat of Edward Braddock. Even the heroic stone monuments at Braddock's Grave and Washington's Fort Necessity are not of this vintage, but were constructed by later generations relative to *their* dictums of interpretation and commemoration. Fort Necessity was actually reconstructed twice. The 1950s fort was pulled down by more recent historians who reinterpreted the site based on new evidence, then rebuilt their own, truer, mockup of the stronghold.

The contest won by the British over the French in 1763 was overturned by the Americans in 1783, opening a new period in which the

Youghiogheny's mountains stood as an impediment to western riches. This preindustrial period of American expansion left an indelible mark across the upper Yough basin when the federal government constructed the National Road between 1811 and 1818. The modern route of U.S. 40 was actually determined by the nature of travel in the early nineteenth century. Foot- and hoof-borne traffic directed by limited road-building budgets favored drainage divide routes where few bridges needed to be built. In this way, the Youghiogheny River was more of a barrier to the National Road than the mountains it drained. Like later automobiles, horse-drawn wagons could handle short, steep slopes better than early engineers could handle the Yough gorges where a roadbed would have had to have been hand-hewn from solid rock and every Yough tributary crossed at its widest point.

To this day, U.S. 40, successor to the National Road, straddles the drainage divide between the Casselman's Whites Creek and the Yough's Mill Run after cresting Meadow Mountain running westbound from Maryland. Where the road builders could not avoid crossing the Yough, they followed in the Roman tradition of erecting heavy stone arches to last the ages, as unable in the early 1800s to see the impending demise of horse travel as the Romans themselves. West of the river, the road finds the divide between Meadow Run and the Monongahela's Big Sandy Creek, staying true to its upland course until Chestnut Ridge, where the Yough Basin is left behind entirely.

The seeds of the Yough's current tourist-oriented landscape were sown primarily in the ash and smoke of its industrial past. Tourism was forged on the anvil of artifice. The same tracks that carried coal and lumber out of the mountains also carried tourists back in, laden with money and leisure time bartered from an expanding industrial economy.

An early plan to industrialize Ohiopyle, or Falls City as it was known until 1881, was an 1825 proposal to make it a national armory. With respect to waterpower, the commissioners wrote that the site "surpassed any that has come under our observation." The idea sputtered, however, due to Ohiopyle's "want of convenient communication surrounded on all sides by mountains, the adjacent country but sparsely settled . . . without means of water conveyance, and, as of yet, without roads." The early industry that appeared to take advantage of unsurpassed waterpower was resource oriented and geared to the local agrarian market, mainly sawmills and gristmills. Albeit small, the mills operated in every sylvan glen cherished by today's nature lovers; on Cucumber Run, near the slides of Meadow Run, at Bear Run, along remote Jonathan Run, and even at Ohiopyle Falls itself, where a water-powered sawmill was later converted to produce hydroelectricity for a while. The vertical drops that make these streams scenic also allowed them to be put to profitable use.

More substantial industry did not arrive until after 1871, when the Pittsburgh and Connellsville Railroad broke Falls City's isolation with its cross-mountain extension to Cumberland. The Baltimore and Ohio (B&O) Railroad purchased the line in 1875. Unlike the wagon-road builders, who traded the high cost of construction through the Yough River gorges for the short, steep grades required to mount the drainage divides, the railroad engineers did not have a choice. A low grade was critical to a mode of travel that struggled with a three-foot climb in a run of a hundred feet. The Yough River route was the only available path for trans-Appalachian railroads building between the Baltimore–Washington DC area and Pittsburgh, regardless of the number or magnitude of the cuts, fills, and bridges needed. Ohiopyle's industrial expansion, like Cumberland's before it, was tied to area timber and coal

Old powerhouse at Ohiopyle Falls on the Youghiogheny River, Fayette County, 1910.

resources, and reliant on railroad access to distant markets. The Falls City Spoke and Hub Works as well as the Falls City Shook Factory (barrel manufacturers) opened four years after the railroad arrived. Thomas Potter's coal mine tapped into the Pittsburgh coal seam in 1877, and the Falls City Pulp Mill began pulping wood for paper in 1879.

In addition to the industrial boom, the railroad was responsible for Falls City's first tourist hotel, the Ohiopyle House, which opened in a remodeled tavern across the tracks from the train station in 1871. In 1879, the fifty-room Ferncliff Hotel opened as a summer resort on Ferncliff Peninsula, the wooded loop of land inside the Yough's meandering curve opposite Falls City. This posh hotel was one of the first

Ohiopyle House hotel in Ohiopyle. Photo by Joseph V. C. White. Courtesy Western Pennsylvania Conservancy.

buildings in town to be electrically lit with power generated by Ohiopyle Falls. The surrounding peninsula was a naturalist's paradise, crisscrossed by winding paths and bordered by the dramatic, rockbound cataracts of the Youghiogheny Loop. To the elite urbanites who stayed at the Ferncliff, the peninsula was a tranquil world of long walks, contemplative vistas, and nightly dances set apart from their hectic lives in the city. Yet the resort experience depended on the railroad running through the serene hills, just as much as the industries of coal mining and logging did.

The railroad put Ohiopyle on the main line of travel between Baltimore–Washington DC and Pittsburgh, drawing summer guests who stayed for days or even weeks at a time. Other resort hotels opened in Ohiopyle and in mountain towns farther up the line such as Rockwood, where the Rockwood House opened for its first summer season in 1882. Summer camps, hunting and fishing clubs, and private second homes dotted the mountains. A few miles down the track from

Ohiopyle was the small B&O station stop at Bear Run, which served Camp Kaufmann. Pittsburgh department store mogul Edgar J. Kaufmann Sr. opened the summer camp on Bear Run for his employees in 1916. Typical of many sylvan retreats strung out along Pennsylvania's mountain rail lines, Camp Kaufmann was popular throughout the 1910s and 1920s, and fell apart in the 1930s.

Ferncliff Hotel about 1920.

The Great Depression expunged this early period of mountain tourism, which faded away along with the passenger trains. Neglected and ailing, the rambling Ferncliff Hotel was torn down in the 1930s. In the rubble, workers found the plumbing that linked the resort's "natural" hot spring—a mainstay of Victorian health-oriented vacations—to the hotel's steam boiler. Ohiopyle and the other mountain hamlets brought to life

by the railroad came to be absorbed by the rural poverty that crept into the hollows of Appalachia after the timber and coal was carted off. The top-hatted and gowned tourists no longer arrived by rail, and the rafters and mass tourism to be carried in on the wheels of the automobile were years away. Ohiopyle lied fallow.

The Youghiogheny River loops around the Ferncliff Peninsula, Ohiopyle State Park, and drops nearly ninety feet in less than two miles. Photograph by Marci McGuiness.

The Great Depression stands as a watershed between the tourism of the Yough's past, which was an outgrowth of rail-oriented, industrial-era resource exploitation; and the tourism of the Yough's

"Bathing along River Front, Ohiopyle, PA." *Swimmers in the Youghiogheny River, above the Falls with the Western Maryland Bridge in the background.* *Courtesy Marci McGuiness.*

automobile-oriented future, which has come to rely on environmental conservation and preservation. A key player in this transition was founded in 1932 as the Greater Pittsburgh Parks Association, whose expressed goal was "to prepare and promote a program for the maintenance, acquisition, development, organization and administration of public parks, parkways, playgrounds, places and facilities for recreation, exercise and games, and, as incidental thereto acquiring, holding and improving real estate and equipment suitable for such parks, parkways, playgrounds, places and facilities." After a slow start, the association began to acquire tracts of land throughout western Pennsylvania for the purpose of nature conservation and recreation, and in 1951 changed its name to the Western Pennsylvania Conservancy. By 1982, the Conservancy had purchased 85,000 acres of land, some of which was transferred to the Commonwealth of Pennsylvania for the creation of five state parks: McConnells Mill, Moraine, Laurel Ridge, Oil Creek, and Ohiopyle. Much of this land had been timbered over and mined out, but under the Conservancy was restored to its natural state, providing the environments that brought a new generation of tourists back into the woods. The Conservancy's mission was compatible with federal New Deal conservation programs and Pennsylvania's state parks program, which set a post–World War II goal of building a park within twenty-five miles of every resident.

The B&O trains quit stopping at Camp Kaufmann in the 1930s, the same decade the road through Kaufmann's property to Ohiopyle, State Route 381, was paved. Camp Kaufmann closed around 1930, but the Kaufmann clan continued to vacation at Bear Run, each family building a summer cottage on the wooded tract and traveling by car to reach it. In 1934, Edgar Sr. invited Frank Lloyd Wright to Bear Run to design what may be the most famous weekend house in America. Cantilevered out over a Bear Run cascade, Fallingwater's stacked terraces were ready for occupation by November 1937. Fallingwater's fame was almost immediate and inspired Kentuck Knob, the ridgetop summer home that Frank Lloyd Wright designed for I. N. Hagan in 1953, which overlooks the Youghiogheny Valley from the south.

Edgar J. Kaufmann would play an instrumental part in the postindustrial recasting of Ohiopyle's identity and fortunes. In 1951, Ferncliff owner Alex Mead was prepared to sell the peninsula to a developer who intended to clear-cut the timber and build an amusement park. In order to preserve Ferncliff's natural quality, Kaufmann bought it and the old Ohiopyle House, and donated both to the Western Pennsylvania Conservancy. The relationship forged in this deal would pave the way for the future preservation of Fallingwater, which Edgar Kaufmann jr would entrust to the Conservancy in 1963.

Ferncliff was the first piece in a 19,052-acre jigsaw puzzle of land purchases that took twenty years to assemble into Ohiopyle State

Park. The Conservancy worked in consort with the state of Pennsylvania to buy the land for the park under Project 70, a program initiated in 1961 to expand the state park system with a $70 million bond issue for land acquisition to be completed by 1970 (thus its name). In the type of clean-sweep planning then popular in urban renewal programs and assisted by the powers of eminent domain, twenty-nine houses were bought and razed in Ohiopyle. The demolitions were largely in the Front Street neighborhood along the river, which was obliterated completely and redesigned into the waterfront park that stands there now. The one unintended loss was Ohiopyle House, which a fire of undetermined origin destroyed in 1964, soon after it had been renovated by the Conservancy. Rumors circulated that it was torched by discontented locals frustrated and angered by the town's dismantling.

High up in the mountains above Confluence, the Youghiogheny River Dam stands as the valley's last major piece of infrastructure built during the industrial period, and the first needed to support the tourist economy that began to bloom as the mines and mills were shutting down. The hammer of industry had seemingly pacified the wild Yough by the early twentieth century. The forces of nature could nonetheless kick up an occasional fuss, particularly when torrential downpours overfilled the Yough and other Ohio River headwater streams with muddy brown water and sent it rushing down on Pittsburgh. Between the first recorded inundation in 1762 and the devastating St. Patrick's Day flood in 1936, Pittsburgh suffered 115 floods that were confirmed by the Army Corps of Engineers as a crest on the Ohio River at least twenty-five feet above normal pool.

Largely located on the floodplains of the city's three rivers, Pittsburgh's expanding railroads, industrial assets, and much of the downtown Golden Triangle stood directly in harm's way every time the river

Fallingwater, designed for Edgar and Liliane Kaufmann by Frank Lloyd Wright. Owned and maintained by the Western Pennsylvania Conservancy, Fallingwater is open to the public year-round. Photograph by Robert P. Ruschak. Courtesy Western Pennsylvania Conservancy.

rose. The Pittsburgh Chamber of Commerce formed the Flood Commission of Pittsburgh in 1908 to combat this threat. Under the leadership of industrialist H. J. Heinz, the commission prepared an unprecedented study, which proposed a basin-wide strategy. Flood control dams would be placed on Allegheny and Monongahela tributaries upstream from Pittsburgh to temporarily store and then gradually release high water, minimizing impact on downstream cities. The plan cast a big shadow, reaching up the Allegheny as far north as New York, east to the crest of the Allegheny Mountains, and south into West Virginia and western Maryland along the Monongahela and its primary tributaries, the Cheat and Youghiogheny rivers. The plan was ambitious and largely ignored by governmental officials. Implementing it took a catastrophic flood and an act of Congress.

Heavy snows and frigid temperatures defined the winter of 1936 for central and western Pennsylvania. Ice dams formed on both the Allegheny and Monongahela rivers, building up and holding back a surge of water that was suddenly released in a late winter thaw. When a deluge of rain mixed with snow arrived on St. Patrick's Day, the rivers were already swollen. Rising, muddy water spilled into the streets of downtown Pittsburgh and did not stop until it reached an astounding depth of forty-six feet. Fires raged out of control, ironically isolated from firefighters by streets turned into watery moats. Thirty-six people died, and 135,000 were forced from their homes.

The 1936 floods were widespread throughout the Northeast. In 1937, Mother Nature drove Pittsburgh's rivers to flood stage six times, and conditions were even worse down the Ohio Valley in Wheeling, Cincinnati, and Louisville. With a Depression-weary New Deal Congress already in a public works mode, federal action followed. The Flood Control Acts of 1936 and 1938 authorized and funded the Army

Aerial view of the Point during the flood of 1936. Photograph from the Pittsburgh Sun-Telegraph. *Courtesy Carnegie Library of Pittsburgh.*

Corps of Engineers to construct and maintain a network of structures, including dams, levees, and floodwalls. In 1937, the Army Corps recommended forty-five reservoirs, including two in the Monongahela Basin's West Virginia headwaters. The Corps was already at work on the Tygart River near Grafton, West Virginia, constructing Tygart Dam, which had been authorized for the purpose of maintaining navigation depths on the upper Monongahela. Local opposition killed a proposed dam on West Fork River, sending the Corps searching for an equally suitable Monongahela tributary. They chose a stretch of wild water on the upper Youghiogheny a little more than a mile above Confluence. The steep-sided, lightly settled valley was located away from the main line of travel marked by the B&O and WM railroads, which followed the Casselman River east of Confluence.

Begun in 1939, construction on the Youghiogheny River Dam was delayed by material shortages during World War II, but the dam was nonetheless ready to capture the 1943 spring freshet and became fully operational by 1948. The dam's weighty presence is felt at all scales. Locally, the 184-foot high, 1,610-foot wide, rock-plated wall of earth and clay has radically transformed the upper Yough Valley, backing up an 83-million-gallon reservoir between the forested shoulders of the surrounding mountains. Stillwater flows over Washington's Great Crossing, and the old towns of Somerfield, Pennsylvania, and Selbysport, Maryland, from which a combined total of 115 buildings were removed. When lake water is drawn down enough, the three-span stone arch bridge built for the National Road in 1818 is exhumed from its watery grave as a ghostly reminder of the past.

In the Laurel and Chestnut ridge gorges, far below the breastworks, the Yough is thrown into its primordial dance of leaping, frothing water, seemingly untouched by the hand of man, but the dam is there pulling the strings. Water held back in the spring tempers a seasonal dance that once ran mad with the excitement of a thawing winter. Water released in the late summer maintains a lively peak performance at a time when the stream formerly slowed to a gentle waltz along a bed that was more rock than river. The role of the Youghiogheny River Dam even transcends the boundaries of its own valley. At the regional scale, it is one of sixteen dams on three river systems that regulate water flowing into the upper Ohio River. All of them are tied to the Army Corps of Engineers command center in Pittsburgh, which makes the decisions to raise and lower the floodgates like so many faucets spilling into the same basin.

Although its primary mission is flood control, the Yough Dam was also designed to assist with pollution abatement through diluting and flushing, which was the traditional method at the time of the dam's creation. Raw sewage from thousands of privies once spilled over the orange-stained rocks of the riverbank and mixed with the acid mine drainage already in the Yough. The effluent was particularly noxious during the low flow weeks of late summer, which is exactly what the summer releases were designed to mitigate. The more effective, albeit challenging, policy currently favored is to treat water pollution at its source with sewage treatment plants and acid mine drainage remediation.

The dam's water releases have had an unintended consequence of laying the foundation for a new Yough economy and identity. Feeling for a route through the mountains in 1754, Washington did not know whether to canoe, raft, or wade the Youghiogheny downstream from Great Crossing. He tried all three, and finally decided to walk around it. Two centuries later, Jean and Sayre Rodman knew what to do with the river. In 1956, they launched two rafts below Ohiopyle Falls, and ran the rapids all the way to Connellsville, pioneering a run they would popularize by guiding other trips down the river. Following in the Rodmans' wake, Lance and Lee Martin and Karl Kruger led the first commercial raft trip on the Yough in 1963. The next year they guided a few hundred people down the river under the name Wilderness Voyageurs, the original river outfitter operating in Ohiopyle. Five thousand people ran the river below Ohiopyle in 1968. Ten years later, that number was 95,000.

Now, four outfitters guide roughly 150,000 tourists down the lower Yough every year, making it the most popular whitewater river in the country. Ohiopyle is home to a fleet of over one thousand boats, including inflatable rafts, canoes, kayaks, and other specialized craft like duckies, yahoos, and shredders. This flotilla sets sail in groups or individually all summer long, joined by countless private crafts. On any given summer Saturday, twenty thousand people may come to visit this village of seventy-two year-round residents. The summer crush of thrill-seeking boaters would (and occasionally does) swamp the tiny town if it were not for a staging area constructed on the edge of town where cars are parked, trips organized, and buses loaded for shuttling to the river put-ins. A single trip can have fifteen rafts or more with four to a boat, plus river guides who herd the hapless with circling kayaks and yell—or sign—instructions from rocky perches poised above the rapids. The potential chaos is limited by regulations that prohibit any additional outfitters from opening shop and caps the combined daily runs at 960 people. On heavy-use days with hundreds of boats on the water, the river runs downhill, the same way that it always has, but the sense of wilderness is lost.

The Yough's popularity in comparison to other whitewater rivers in Appalachia is largely due to its size, commodious enough to handle big trips; its diverse hydrology, providing everything from gentle float trips to life-threatening Class V rapids; and especially water releases from the Yough River Dam, which extend the rafting season long after most other rivers have shut down for the summer due to seasonal low water. Whitewater rafting has redefined the identity of the Yough. To colonial troop movements, trade, and transportation, it was a watery barrier. To industrial-age railroads, it was the trans-Appalachian path of least resistance. To modern-day tourists, it is a leisure-time highway to adventure. As a highway, the river is governed by rules, posted with signs, and populated with place names, all very real on the boater's map, but invisible to the casual observer gazing out on a scenic, wild river seemingly unchanged since before the time of man.

The boatable river is divided into three sections. The vicious upper Yough is in Maryland above the lake, and can only be run during the high water season by experts. The placid middle Yough between Confluence and Ohiopyle is open to all boaters, and includes some moderate rapids within the Laurel Ridge. The wild and scenic lower Yough

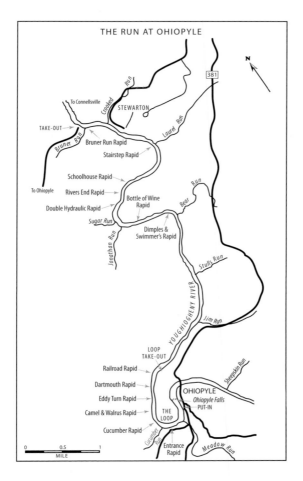

THE RUN AT OHIOPYLE

To Connellsville

STEWARTON

TAKE-OUT

Bruner Run Rapid

Stairstep Rapid

Schoolhouse Rapid

To Ohiopyle   Rivers End Rapid

Double Hydraulic Rapid

Bottle of Wine Rapid

Sugar Run

Dimples & Swimmer's Rapid

LOOP TAKE-OUT

Railroad Rapid

Dartmouth Rapid

Eddy Turn Rapid

Camel & Walrus Rapid

Cucumber Rapid

OHIOPYLE

Ohiopyle Falls

PUT-IN

THE LOOP

Entrance Rapid

0   0.5   1
MILE

The run at Ohiopyle. Map adapted from the River Guide for Youghiogheny River *by Tim Palmer.*

carries the most traffic; it has a put-in just below Ohiopyle Falls, and a take-out at Bruner Run beyond the gorge through Chestnut Ridge. The shortest run is the first mile and a half of the lower Yough, known as the Loop because it covers most of a rapid-packed incised meandering curve around Ferncliff Peninsula. From the High Bridge take-out, it is only a short walk across the neck of the peninsula to reach the upstream Yough at the point it enters the Loop above the Falls.

For guided trips, the rules of the river are given to each gang of boats before putting in. Safety is emphasized and despite the carnival atmosphere, people are reminded that the Yough is not an amusement park ride. The river claims on average one life every year, but no one on a guided trip has ever drowned. The rules are conveyed through simple, even primitive, hand gestures. Stop. Go. Paddle right. Paddle left. And the dreaded Get down in the boat. This means you are about to go over the rapids in an uncontrolled way and there is nothing you can do about it. When swept overboard, point your feet downstream, let the current take you to a safe place to be pulled back in the boat, and never, never try to stand in whitewater. Feet can become hopelessly jammed in underwater crevices, making rescue difficult, if not impossible.

The river is without printed signs, but well-recognized rocks and water channels point the proper path through each set of rapids. Stay to the left of Sugarloaf Rock at Entrance Rapids. At Cucumber Rapids, run the chute close to Table Rock, and don't get caught on Mr. Edwards, an undercut ledge where a man by that name drowned. Run between the Camel and the Walrus at normal flow, but sail over the back of the Walrus during high water for a better ride. A gravel bar on the right bank announces the approach of Dimple Rock sitting at the base of a Class III rapid that has taken two lives. Even the soaring Western Maryland High Bridge is a sign. This is the place where Loopers, those running only the Loop, pull out of the river.

Distance on the linear world of the river is marked by rapids, each named with some reference to its christening event or location, each with its own character and identity. The rapids come in quick succession in the Loop: Entrance, Cucumber (at the mouth of Cucumber

Run), Camel and Walrus, Dartmouth (where that college holds slalom kayak races in the fall), and Railroad (in the shadow of High Bridge). High Bridge is the gateway to the Doldrums, a two-mile stretch of gentle water before the next series of rapids: Dimple, Swimmers, Bottle of Wine (memorializing a half-bottle of wine found on a rock), Double Hydraulic (a hole where the river rolls back on itself, twice), and Bruner Run Rapid, which signals the end of the seven-mile run.

Years ago, passengers shuttling back and forth on the WM and B&O railroads stared out the windows, catching glimpses of blue-green water through the trees and occasional splashes of nameless white rapids. Now, thousands of river runners paddling away the dog days of summer are intimately familiar with these well-known rapids, and occasionally look up to catch glimpses of anonymous passing CSX trains.

The final piece in Ohiopyle's postindustrial puzzle came with the conversion of the Western Maryland Railway's right-of-way into one of the most ambitious rails-to-trails projects in the country. Contrary to popular perception, America's railroads were not made obsolete by the automobile and then subsequently abandoned. They were, however, radically transformed and forced to redefine their niche in the nation's transportation system.

In 1912, the WM completed a line that paralleled B&O's main line from Baltimore to Pittsburgh by way of a connection with the Pittsburgh and Lake Erie Railroad at Connellsville. After 1931, the Pittsburgh and West Virginia Railway connected to the WM at Connellsville, and linked with the Nickel Plate Road (the New York, Chicago, and St. Louis Railroad line) to Chicago. This so-called Alphabet Route provided an alternate passage between the Midwest and New York City. Constructed forty-two years before, the B&O line had the choice of grades, commandeering Wills Creek Valley west from Cumberland and the Sand Patch

Grade to a tunnel beneath Meadow Mountain at the crest of the Allegheny Plateau. The downhill run to Pittsburgh, still traveled by CSX trains today, follows the right bank of the Casselman and Yough rivers to the Monongahela Valley. Forced to carve a more difficult route, the late-arriving Western Maryland had the advantage of more advanced technology, allowing heavier grades, deeper cuts and larger bridges to produce a superior grade. The route crested the Alleghenies at Big Savage Tunnel, and then descended to the P&LE link at Connellsville, largely keeping to the left banks of the Casselman and Yough.

In an age of active coal mines and poor highways, the traffic supported the redundant competitive routes, but as the market for rail movements declined, stronger roads absorbed the weaker roads. In 1963, the C&O bought stock in the Baltimore and Ohio, and in 1964, the combined C&O/B&O filed with the Interstate Commerce Commission for permission to acquire Western Maryland. Then, in 1973, the C&O and B&O lines came together with the WM and became the Chessie System. In 1975, all Western Maryland through trains were rerouted over the paralleling B&O tracks between Connellsville and the Potomac Valley at Big Pool Junction, Maryland, leaving the abandoned line to weed over. The WM tracks were removed from the Yough Valley in the 1980s, as were the P&LE tracks north of Connellsville. Although apparently dead, the discarded right-of-way was actually in a dormant chrysalis state, awaiting rebirth.

Railroads were not the only redundant elements in the region's industrial economy. By the end of the 1980s, six out of seven integrated steel mills in the Mon Valley had shut down for good, their silent hulks awaiting only the cutter's torch and the sweep of the bulldozer blade. Many other factories were shuttered as well. After the dust settled, politicians and planners picked through the industrial debris for bits and

The Cumberland and Pennsylvania Railroad tracks were adjacent to the C&O Canal so coal could be easily loaded onto canal boats. Courtesy City of Cumberland, Herman and Stacia Miller Collection.

Western Maryland Railroad Station at Ohiopyle. Courtesy Marci McGuiness.

pieces of infrastructure that could be refashioned into something useful in a world no longer ruled by coal, coke, iron, and steel.

Public-private partnerships, grants, donations, and volunteer-assisted nonprofit organizations have redrawn the map of southwestern Pennsylvania. Traditionally ignored in Pennsylvania's pragmatic industrial landscapes, conservation and historic preservation have become founding principles to recent economic (re)development. Former coal basins and mill valleys knitted together by railroads have faded beneath a map of heritage areas and watershed associations reliant on an infrastructure of bike paths, hiking trails, and historic highway circuits.

The entire route from Cumberland to Pittsburgh has been reinvented as the Great Allegheny Passage, a 150-mile bike path built and maintained by six different trail associations collectively organized as the Allegheny Trail Alliance (ATA). (A seventh trail organization, the Montour Trail Council, also belongs to the ATA. The forty-six-mile Montour Trail runs west of Pittsburgh, terminating at Clairton, a few miles south of the Great Allegheny Passage in McKeesport.) The low grades so carefully engineered to accommodate heavy trains on the fast freight line through the mountains have proven to be perfect for pedaling a bicycle through miles of auto-free forests. Although the path attains an elevation of 2,375 feet at the crest of the Alleghenies, the slope never exceeds 2 percent.

The Three Rivers Heritage Trail manages the first leg of the Great Allegheny Passage, which follows the left bank of the Monongahela River upstream from its confluence with the Allegheny and Ohio rivers in Pittsburgh. Fittingly enough, the trail starts at the former terminal yards of the Pittsburgh and Lake Erie Railroad, and ends six miles up the river, near the site of the now closed Mesta Machine works. The previous occupants of these endpoints represent old Pittsburgh. The current occupants, Station Square mall and entertainment complex and Sandcastle Waterpark, are indicative of the changes that have occurred all along the route.

Pittsburgh's economic transformation is nearly complete. With one exception, the great steel mills of the Mon Valley are but a memory kept alive through the efforts of the Rivers of Steel National Heritage Area, one of a dozen heritage areas across Pennsylvania that have emerged from the remains of the state's industrial past since the creation of the Pennsylvania Heritage Parks Program in 1990. The program recognized that the state's industrial heritage could be preserved and showcased for economic and community development while stimulating opportunities for recreation, education, and cultural conservation. The industries that were targeted were iron and steel, coal, textiles, machinery and foundry, transportation, lumber, oil, and agriculture—nearly the same list of economic sectors suffering the most from deindustrialization. The contraction of these industries created the very preservation opportunities the program hoped to stimulate as an unprecedented number of industrial sites were abandoned.

The Steel Valley Trail runs through the heart of the heritage area from Sandcastle to the mouth of the Yough in McKeesport. U.S. Steel's mammoth Homestead Works, near the trail's northern terminus, was demolished around 1990. In its place, a suburban-like, mixed-used development known as The Waterfront has risen. The old plate mill's row of brick stacks tower above the restaurants, theaters, and shopping centers as a detached, postmodern monument to the not too distant, smoky past. Along the riverbank, the old pump house and water tank have been preserved at the site where the Pinkerton Agency unsuccessfully attempted to unload barges of strikebreakers in the face of angry steelworkers in 1892.

On the opposite shore, the Carrie Furnaces loom above the trees that have taken root along the river since the silencing of Vulcan's hammer. Though silent and cold, the intact row includes a pair of blast furnaces separated by a row of gas stoves standing before an ore pit and bridge and connected to the casting house. A perfect example of an integrated steel mill's "hot end," the Carrie Furnaces received National Historic Landmark status in 2006 and are the object of a preservation and museum initiative that will turn them into the centerpiece museum of the National Heritage Area. The Hot Metal Bridge used to carry molten iron from the blast furnaces to the steel furnaces and fabricating shops on the Homestead side of the river will one day carry pedestrians and bicyclists between the two redeveloped sites.

The Steel Valley Trail runs along the opposite bank of the Monongahela River from U.S. Steel's Edgar Thomson works, still throbbing as both the first and the last integrated steel mill in the valley. It follows the route of a former U.S. Steel gas pipeline located on the hillside below Kennywood amusement park and then skirts the fringes of an industrial park built on the site of the former Duquesne Works before crossing over the Riverton Bridge to McKeesport, where it edges along the former National Tube Works, also redeveloped as an industrial park. The trail continues through Glassport and on to Clairton, where the world's largest by-product coke plant still turns out its product among smoke, steam, and flame.

The Steel Valley Trail intersects the Youghiogheny River Trail at the McKees Point Park confluence of the Yough and Mon. The Youghiogheny River Trail North follows the P&LE's right-of-way upstream to Connellsville, where it meets the Youghiogheny River Trail, which uses the Western Maryland's right-of-way into the Allegheny Mountains. The trail bisects the Connellsville Coke District, which sits in the synclinal basin immediately west of and parallel to the anticlinal Chestnut Ridge. This was a world-class coal and coke area in terms of value and production, and both Fayette and Westmoreland counties have the scars to prove it.

Although most mines were abandoned long ago, some coal mines still operate throughout the region. These mines, combined with the abandoned mines and their spoil piles, continue to present the area's

*The Carrie Furnaces,
part of the Homestead
Steel Works, were built in
1884 and they operated
until 1982. Courtesy
Rivers of Steel National
Heritage Area.*

*Relic of the Carrie
Furnaces, viewed from
the Monongahela River.
Courtesy Rivers of Steel
National Heritage Area.*

greatest ecological challenge. Water flowing over exposed coal, whether groundwater in an abandoned deep mine or rainwater runoff through a waste bony pile, leaches iron oxides, aluminum, and manganese into streams, lowering the pH to such unlivable levels as to create aquatic deserts. Streams suffering from severe acid mine drainage have been tainted a telltale orange by the iron oxides that precipitate out and coat the rocks, river bottom, and anything else in the water. Unless clouded with a heavy sediment load, a by-product of strip mining, the acidic waters run amazingly clear, because no plant life can live in them, ensuring that more complex life forms—macro-invertebrates and fish—will have no food source.

The region's acidic, orange-colored streams are an obvious detriment to an economy based in recreation and tourism, and have therefore come under recent scrutiny through the creation of state and federally funded public watershed associations charged with restoring health to mine-polluted waters. The Department of Conservation and Natural Resources maintains no less than five river conservation programs within the Youghiogheny watershed, covering Laurel Hill Creek, the Casselman River, Indian Creek, Sewickley Creek, and the Yough itself.

In the 1880s, the Yough's hills and hollows were scoured for places to lay track to gain access to the Pittsburgh coal seam. Collieries, coal patch towns, and coke ovens followed. One hundred years later, the National Park Service canvassed the hills and hollows again to survey what was left of the built environment assembled to get the coal and coke out. The resulting *Reconnaissance Survey of Western Pennsylvania Roads and Sites* laid the foundation for the federally funded Southwestern Pennsylvania Heritage Preservation Commission, which was formed in 1989 to reinvent the identity of a nine-county area. For the first time, humble villages like Dawson and Star Junction were re-

Riverton Bridge, formerly owned by the Union Railroad, over the Monongahela River at McKeesport. Courtesy Rivers of Steel National Heritage Area.

viewed as monuments to the working-class populations who devoted their lives to toil in the mines and at the ovens of industry. In some places, the environmental mitigation programs have been at cross-purposes with historic preservation, tearing out scores of beehive coke ovens and pulling down coal processing plants as part of a reclamation that returns landscapes of industrial heritage to a presettlement state of open fields with little left to interpret.

The commission laid out and marked an extensive and circuitous Southwestern Pennsylvania Industrial Heritage Route, or Path of Progress, over the region's highways to import tourists into a region historically renowned for its mineral and manufacturing exports. In its sweep through Westmoreland and Fayette counties, the Path of Progress crosses the Youghiogheny at Connellsville, where the region's first successful beehive coke oven operated, and where the mansions of the old coal and coke barons still line Pittsburgh Street as testimony to how the other half lived.

Upstream in Ohiopyle, the millennium brought new construction to a Western Maryland right-of-way that had been dormant for decades. Fresh gravel was laid, and new spans were swung onto the piers of the Yough River bridge. Of course, the intended mode was bicycle, the Western Maryland trains having been relegated to old photographs on the walls of the former depot, restored as the Ohiopyle Visitors Center. At Confluence, the Youghiogheny River Trail links with the Allegheny Highlands Trail to follow in the footsteps of the Western Maryland up the Casselman River, over the Allegheny summit, and down the steep eastern edge of the Allegheny Plateau to Cumberland.

The Allegheny Highlands Trail showcases the Western Maryland Railway's ingenuity in the face of difficult mountain topography. The leveling of the route is in part achieved by feats of railroad engineering, such as the 1,908-foot long Salisbury Viaduct spanning the Casselman Valley north of Meyersdale, a spectacular ride and popular draw for bikers. The hard pull for eastbound trains began at the Salisbury Viaduct where the grade stiffened through Meyersdale and up to the Eastern Continental Drainage Divide near Deal. The bike path crosses the Keystone Viaduct just west of the paralleling CSX line's Sand Patch Tunnel, which still resounds with the thunder of frequent freight trains. The Western Maryland's Allegheny summit tunnel pierced Big Savage Mountain at the crest of the grade. More than $12 million in grants were secured from the state and foundations to reconstruct the Big Savage Tunnel and make it suitable for biking. At 3,300 feet, this bore is the longest tunnel on any bike path in the state.

South of the Mason-Dixon Line, the Allegheny Highlands Trail of Maryland includes the 945-foot long Borden Tunnel. East of Frostburg, the path runs along-side the Western Maryland Scenic Railroad, ten miles of active Western Maryland right-of-way that have been retained

to tote tourists between Frostburg and Cumberland behind what is now perceived as the romantic glory of steam power. Both tourist train and bike path follow Brush Tunnel through a spur of Piney Mountain, and are then enveloped by the high rock walls of the Narrows, a steep-sided water gap through Wills Mountain that historically functioned as Cumberland's gateway to the West.

Cumberland prospered as the industrial-age interface between rail and canal, especially for eastbound coal from the Allegheny Mountains. With the completion of the Great Allegheny Passage, eastbound bikers coming out of the mountains interface with the Chesapeake and Ohio Canal towpath at the restored Western Maryland Railway Station, a symbolic juncture in time and space. The station was built in 1910 on the filled-in site of the original terminal canal basin. It now serves the Western Maryland Scenic Railroad.

THE SPIRIT OF THE PASSAGE   233

The rise, fall, and reincarnation of the Chesapeake and Ohio (C&O) Canal followed a similar trajectory as the Western Maryland Railway, only sooner. An 1889 flood devastated the financially wracked canal, putting it into receivership and allowing it to be taken over by its largest shareholder, the Baltimore and Ohio Railroad. Even though the faster, more reliable, and profitable B&O paralleled the bankrupt canal for nearly its entire length, the company kept the channel open. The C&O was still serviceable for bulk commodities like coal, which could move more cheaply by water at a slower pace, freeing track space for more profitable cargo. It took another flood, in 1924, to close the canal for good. By this time, the Western Maryland Railway had opened, doubling the capacity for trans-Appalachian rail movements through Cumberland. Ultimately, the B&O bought, and subsequently abandoned both the WM and the C&O Canal.

The National Park Service purchased the 185-mile C&O Canal in 1938, planning to use it for a new parkway similar to the Blue Ridge Parkway then being built. Before construction could begin, however, World War II interceded. By the time the issue resurfaced in the 1950s, the moment had passed. Exhibiting insight decades ahead of his time, U.S. Supreme Court Justice William O. Douglas set out to derail the parkway plan in 1954, favoring instead conservation and historic preservation. In March 1954, he challenged the editors of the *Washington Post* and Baltimore's *Evening Sun* to join him on a full-length hike of the canal from Cumberland to Georgetown to see for themselves what the new highway would destroy. The challenge was accepted, and the media coverage that followed garnered the support that would redefine the corridor as sacred space.

In 1971, the Chesapeake and Ohio Canal was christened a national historical park. Improvements to the towpath followed, as well

NORTH BRANCH LOCK
C.&O.CANAL

25-483   Year 1909

A barge passes through the C&O Canal locks. Courtesy City of Cumberland, Herman and Stacia Miller Collection.

as other amenities like visitor centers, interpretive sites, and the rewatering of small stretches of canal in order to float reconstructed canal boats. The historical park was created one year before the C&O Railroad took over the Western Maryland Railway, and four years before the WM's Yough Valley line was abandoned. When 1980s deindustrialization swept through southwestern Pennsylvania, shedding redundant infrastructure, the C&O Canal Historical Park already existed as a model of conservation, historic preservation, and heritage tourism. A rebuilt, hikeable, bikeable towpath was already reaching out to the foot of the Alleghenies, just like the wagon roads, canals, railroads and auto roads before it, and the path over the mountains to Pittsburgh was becoming clear. At the dawning of the twenty-first century, Americans had once again returned to the Great Allegheny Passage to conquer the mountains with infrastructure suitable to the desires and demands of their time period.

Most Pittsburghers would readily recognize Ohiopyle and the Allegheny Mountains as being nearly synonymous with vacation. It conjures up images of summer; camping beneath a forest canopy, whitewater rafting, mountain hikes and bike rides, cool waterfalls, and historic attractions. The easy association is affirmation of a landscape converted. It is a landscape of leisure recreation and tourism in which previous landscapes are embedded and through which they are interpreted. The visitor bureaus have repackaged Ohiopyle, the entire Youghiogheny River basin, and points beyond as part of the Laurel Highlands, a region encompassing the parallel mountain crests of Allegheny, Laurel, and Chestnut ridges. The presettlement forest primeval is experienced not exactly as a trackless, virgin wilderness, but through its modern equivalent—restored and protected within state parks, state forests, and a dozen tracts acquired by the Western Pennsylvania Conservancy. Nearly a dozen Youghiogheny River outfitters turn what was a harrowing challenge for frontiersmen into vacation fun, and four different mountain resorts call winter visitors into the highlands to ski.

In the Laurel Highlands, the Seven Years' War is not so much a series of historical events as it is a set of historic sites best represented at Jumonville Glen, Braddock's Grave, Fort Ligonier, and Fort Necessity National Battlefield. The National Road Heritage Corridor, following U.S. Route 40 from Cumberland through Uniontown and Washington to Wheeling, preserves a built environment dating to the crash of the first wave of westward migration against the ramparts of the Alleghenies. The Lincoln Highway Heritage Corridor crossing the mountains farther north along U.S. Route 30 celebrates a different frontier

William O. Douglas on the C&O Canal path. Courtesy C&O Canal National Historical Park.

period, when the earliest automobiles were wending their way along America's first transcontinental highway. In addition, the entire industrial age is strung out along the Great Allegheny Passage in the towns, tunnels, canals, bridges, remnant mills, and mines built along the trans-Appalachian rail corridor between Pittsburgh and the Atlantic tidewater cities of Washington DC and Baltimore.

A river runs through this layering of mountainous landscapes, representing the rise and fall of empires, the expansion and contraction of industry, and the conservation and restoration of nature. This river is the twenty-first century Yough.

Pinkerton Low Bridge over Casselman River near Markleton.

(right) Pinkerton High Bridge over Casselman River near Fort Hill.

(left) Fall, from the Pinkerton High Bridge.

Summer on the Great Allegheny Passage near Harnedsville.

(left) *Keystone Viaduct near Meyersdale.*

Restored Western Maryland Railway Station at Meyersdale.

Casselman River and wind turbine just north of Garrett.

THE GREAT ALLEGHENY PASSAGE TRAIL

A Community Effort

PAUL G WIEGMAN

On May 21, 1975, a small train rolled out of the Baltimore and Ohio (B&O) Railroad Station in Pittsburgh. At the head was a yellow, red, and blue locomotive, #6600, with the image of a sleeping kitten painted on the side. It belonged to the recently formed Chessie System, under which the Chesapeake and Ohio (C&O) Railway, the Baltimore and Ohio (B&O) Railway, and the Western Maryland (WM) Railway had been consolidated in 1973. The Chessie car was followed by a gleaming, stainless steel Amtrak Silver Dome, #9401, and a vintage blue, white, red, and silver Western Maryland coach, #1700. The passengers, a diverse group of local officials, conservation organization officers, and press and television reporters, were anticipating a historic ride. They had been invited on the last passenger train to ply the route of the scheduled-to-be-abandoned Western Maryland Railway, from the Bowest Yards near Connellsville, Pennsylvania, to Cumberland, Maryland.

The excursion was a promotional ride arranged by WM executives

Last train on the Western Maryland Railway waiting at the former B&O station in Pittsburgh, May 21, 1975. Photograph by Paul g Wiegman.

and the Western Pennsylvania Conservancy. The purpose was to provide a firsthand look at the route along the exceptionally scenic path of the WM through the Allegheny Mountains, across the Eastern Continental Divide, to the edge of the Ridge and Valley Province, and on to the Potomac River.

After more than seventy years of carrying freight and passengers, the Western Maryland was about to cease operations. Interstate highways had increased the transport of people and goods between cities by road, and the demise of the WM was one more casualty in the continuing shrinkage of railroads during the 1950s and 1960s.

The line between Cumberland and Connellsville through the Allegheny Mountains followed the easiest grade possible, through the mountains, not over them. That route was confined to the deep valleys carved by the Casselman and Youghiogheny rivers. Since the B&O had secured the east and north side of the Casselman from Meyersdale to Confluence and the Youghiogheny from Confluence to Connellsville, the WM used land on the west and south side of the same rivers. When it became apparent in the 1970s that the operation of two rail lines through the Allegheny Mountains with mirrored tracks on either side of the rivers was no longer profitable, and since the B&O lines had been upgraded, it was the WM that was slated to be abandoned.

Western Maryland management was proud of its railway and was fully aware of the exceptional scenic qualities of the route through the mountains of western Maryland and southwestern Pennsylvania. WM executives wanted to make sure that the scenic right-of-way, almost wholly owned by the railroad, would change from a route of steam power to one of human power. They envisioned a public trail replacing the tracks between Cumberland and Connellsville, the western terminus of the railway. With this vision, they approached the National Park Service, hoping that the railway route could become a national park. The reception to this idea, however, was lukewarm.

Western Maryland management then contacted other national and local conservation groups with the same idea. However, the complexity of owning and managing a narrow, linear park of over 150 miles through remote and rugged terrain was daunting. Group after group declined the offer.

In 1972, WM executives approached the Western Pennsylvania Conservancy, a land trust based in Pittsburgh. During the 1960s, the Conservancy, working with Pennsylvania State Parks, had acquired much of the land for McConnells Mill, Oil Creek, Moraine, and Ohiopyle State Parks. The Conservancy was also instrumental in assembling the bits and pieces of land to build the Laurel Highlands Hiking Trail, a seventy-mile long backpacking trail following the summit of Laurel Ridge in the Allegheny Mountains. The president of the Western Pennsylvania Conservancy at the time was Joshua Whetzel Jr., who, when working for the Conservation Foundation in Washington, became familiar with the C&O Canal Towpath and knew the value of long trails through spectacular landscapes. Whetzel fervently embraced the notion of a trail to be built on the Western Maryland route. The Conservancy accepted the offer and the challenge.

The usual arrangement for Conservancy projects was to acquire suitable wild land then find a public agency that would develop the property for recreation and hold it in perpetuity. The obvious third partner for the Western Maryland Project, the original name of what would later become the Great Allegheny Passage, was the Commonwealth of Pennsylvania.

Before the project could begin in earnest, the WM had to officially abandon the railroad. The process began with a petition to the Interstate Commerce Commission (ICC) on June 11, 1973. Although the WM made a strong economic case based on duplication of service and inefficiency, there was opposition. One voice arguing against abandonment was Pennsylvania governor Milton J. Shapp (1971–1979), who was generally concerned about the loss of rail lines throughout Pennsylvania, not particularly the WM petition.

The governor's office publicly testified against abandonment of the Western Maryland Railway. The Pennsylvania Department of Environmental Resources (DER, later the Department of Conservation and Natural Resources, DCNR) and the Pennsylvania Department of Transportation (PennDOT) were in favor of the abandonment. In Ohiopyle, Confluence, and Rockwood, WM bridges and bridge piers were bottlenecks along heavily used highways. Abandonment of the railway would allow the obstructions to be removed, and large trucks could pass more easily into the small towns.

During public hearings, the WM presented a strong case, which included the intention to make its land available for a public hiking and biking trail. Mr. George M. Leilich, vice president of the Western Maryland, closed his testimony by noting how the right-of-way bisected Ohiopyle State Park, land which the Conservancy already planned to acquire. He stated, "Instead of the railroad track cutting through the park, there will be an eighteen-mile nature and bicycle pathway." This was the first public reference to a bike trail following the Western Maryland Railway right-of-way. The Conservancy reinforced the notion with its own testimony and a promise to do what it could to carry out the project.

In the end, the petition for abandonment of the Western Maryland Railway was granted by the ICC on February 14, 1975. Almost immediately, the Western Pennsylvania Conservancy began to plan for a special train ride to be held on May 21, 1975. The last train to Cumberland left the station early that morning. The day was sunny, and spring was in full leaf and flower. The passengers were excited to be on a train, an experience that was becoming rarer and rarer in 1975, and especially to be on a historic train. From Pittsburgh to Connellsville, the route followed tracks along the Monongahela River. At McKeesport, Pennsylvania, the train turned and hugged the banks of the Youghio-

Press briefing in the Bowest Yards of the Western Maryland Railway near Dunbar. Photograph by Paul g Wiegman.

gheny River. On the opposite side of the river, riders could see the still-operational Pennsylvania and Lake Erie Railroad (P&LE).

In Connellsville, while a complicated process of switching to the Western Maryland line was taking place, the passengers gathered in the Bowest Railroad Yards for a press conference, during which the Western Pennsylvania Conservancy publicly presented the Western Maryland Project for the first time. After hearing about the spectacular wild beauty of the Western Maryland route through the Allegheny Mountains between Connellsville and Cumberland, passengers re-boarded and experienced it firsthand.

The train pulled out of the yards and headed upstream along the south side of the wild and frothy Youghiogheny River. The fresh green of the forest glowed in the spring sun and the blue water was punctuated with the sparking white churn of the rapids in the valley below which could be heard even above the muffled roar of the locomotive.

Right before Ohiopyle, Pennsylvania, at the end of Bridge #237.9 —a girder-plate structure 663 feet long and 90 feet above the Youghiogheny River, just downstream of Railroad Rapids—the train stopped. Passengers who had the nerve walked across the railing-less span to the other side, where they got a chance to watch and photograph the

Passengers waiting for the last train to cross Bridge #237.9, now the Ohiopyle High Bridge. Photograph by Paul g Wiegman.

last passenger train to cross. That bridge is now called the Ohiopyle High Bridge and is one of the most popular destinations on the Great Allegheny Passage for both cyclists and walkers.

Once passengers and train were on the Ohiopyle side of the bridge, passengers resumed their seats. Because PennDOT had been so efficient in getting a span removed from the Ohiopyle Low Bridge so trucks could more easily pass, the train had to switch over to the B&O side of the river. The detour continued to Confluence. At the Transfer Flats between Confluence and Harnedsville, the train got back on the WM tracks and continued to Cumberland, Maryland.

The route was highlighted by a uniquely curved and banked bridge over the Casselman River at Harnedsville, passage through the Pinkerton Tunnel, and a bridge that spanned the Casselman River between Fort Hill and Markleton. In Rockwood, Pennsylvania, a gentleman waited near the tracks crossing Rockwood Road. His name was Maynard Stembower. He was noticeable among other longtime Rockwood residents watching the last train because Maynard had stood near the same spot sixty-three years before and watched the first train on the Western Maryland. Later in the 1990s, Maynard saw the beginning of another era and another mode of transportation along the right-of way, when the first section of the bicycle trail (then called Allegheny Highlands Trail) opened from Rockwood to Garrett on June 4, 1994, appropriately National Trails Day. In 2008, Maynard Stembower is nearing the century mark and is still very much a part of the Great Allegheny Passage. He greets visitors, offers sage advice, and continues to spend his summer days at the Great Allegheny Passage Trail Access Visitors' Center in Rockwood.

After Rockwood, passengers on the train enjoyed the iconic Salisbury and Keystone viaducts on either side of Meyersdale, Pennsylvania. Just after crossing the Eastern Continental Divide at over 2,300 feet above sea level, they then rolled into the soot black of the 3,300-foot Big Savage Tunnel. Emerging from the darkness on the southeastern side, the crystal clear breathtaking vista of the Ridge and Valley Province was a sharp contrast. From there, the trip down the Allegheny Front to the Potomac River at Cumberland was an easy twenty or so miles for the train.

The point of this journey was to introduce would-be supporters to the idea of a biking/hiking trail to take the place of the rails. Judging by the enthusiasm of the riders the journey was a huge success. They talked about the spectacular scenery, the sinuous ride along free-flowing rivers, the deep forests, and the surrounding mountains. Not only were the passengers excited about the possibilities, they were ready to begin building the trail, seemingly the next day. When one of

*The former Western
Maryland Railway bridge
over U.S. Route 40 near
Cumberland, Maryland.
Photograph by Paul g
Wiegman.*

the riders was asked by a *New York Times* reporter how long it would take to have such a trail in place, he answered, optimistically, "a year or two."

Back in the offices of the Western Pennsylvania Conservancy the detail work began the very next day. Aside from the myriad of real estate details involved with sorting out seventy-five-year-old acquisition records along 116.55 miles of right-of-way, one significant problem began to emerge. Hesitation on the part of Pennsylvania DER, especially the Bureau of State Parks, was becoming evident. The Bureau of Parks would ultimately be responsible for developing the trail and maintaining and protecting the land. It is easier to oversee a 1,000-acre park centered in a single area than to stretch those 1,000 acres out to 66 feet wide and 116 miles long. The management becomes a nightmare, especially in remote areas where access is limited.

Another looming problem was the preservation and maintenance of structures. The route included two major tunnels, the Big Savage and the Pinkerton; two viaducts, the Keystone and Salisbury; and eight major bridges, two over the Casselman at the Pinkerton Horn, one at Harnedsville, two at Confluence (one of which had a span already missing), two at Ohiopyle (also one with a span missing), and one over Dunbar Creek near Connellsville. The bridges would require few repairs at the time of abandonment, but over the long life of the intended trail would need regular and expensive maintenance.

In addition, the Water Obstructions Act of 1913 clearly stated that if a bridge or other structure over a stream was abandoned, the owner was required to remove said structure if it was not rehabilitated for another use. The deadline for such transformation was short, and there was a possibility that one arm of state government would force another to spend millions to seal tunnels and demolish bridges.

The Conservancy's plan was to acquire the Western Maryland right-of-way and hold it until such time that the state could find the money for purchase. This shifted the potential responsibility of sealing tunnels and removing bridges into the hands of the Conservancy. After long discussions with legal counsel, that possibility was considered to be one that could bankrupt the relatively small, nonprofit Conservancy.

Not to be deterred, Joshua Whetzel and John Oliver, then vice president of the Conservancy, set out to investigate all the possibilities for putting the right-of-way to some use in addition to biking/hiking, thus avoiding the necessity of removing the tunnels and bridges. Gas and oil transmission pipeline companies, electrical transmission lines, long-distance telephone services, logging companies, and others were contacted. What made the Western Maryland the perfect route for a trail—the fact that it traversed long sections of wild, remote land far from major centers of population—made it less than perfect for channeling energy, communications, and resources.

The Commonwealth of Pennsylvania, in the mean time, embraced the idea of acquiring the Western Maryland land within the existing boundaries of Ohiopyle State Park and a bit beyond, given present needs and anticipating some expansion. A counterproposal to acquiring the whole 116 miles of the right-of-way was a far smaller purchase of land extending from the Fayette County side of the bridge over the Youghiogheny River at Confluence to near Connellsville—around twenty-five miles. The Confluence end was considered to be an extension of the park at which a new entrance could be constructed, since Ohiopyle was becoming crowded with rafting, hikers, and sightseers.

During Conservancy negotiations with the state, the Western Maryland Railway remained adamant about transferring the whole line, and its board of directors passed resolutions to allow that to happen. The Western Pennsylvania Conservancy was in the middle, supporting the acquisition of the whole line, but dogged by the possibility of holding bridges that it could be made to demolish at great cost.

Ultimately the state held fast and the Conservancy, with great reluctance, scaled back the project and notified the Western Maryland Railway that its purchase would be land from Confluence to Bowest. In a letter from Joshua Whetzel to Robert Hintz of the Chessie System, the company that now owned the Western Maryland property, Whetzel voiced disappointment that the vision so welcomed by so many on the train in 1975 would have to be limited to a smaller project, but that the result would protect some of the best parts of the route.

Western Maryland Railway over the Casselman River at Confluence. Photograph by Paul g Wiegman.

In June 1978, the Conservancy purchased fifteen miles of Western Maryland right-of-way within and beyond the north and south of Ohiopyle State Park. The reason behind the purchase was primarily to assure that other interests would not acquire the land and develop facilities that would compromise the scenic and ecologic integrity of this outstanding landscape.

Five months later, in November 1978, the Conservancy held a small ceremony in the parking lot of Ferncliff Peninsula, just a few hundred feet from where passengers on the last train in 1975 had cheered the crossing of the high bridge, to mark the sale of that fifteen-mile tract by WPC to the Pennsylvania Bureau of State Parks. Attendees at

John C. Oliver, president of the Western Pennsylvania Conservancy, presenting the title for the former Western Maryland Railway land through Ohiopyle State Park to officials from the Bureau of State Parks in the Ferncliff Peninsula parking lot. Photograph by Paul g Wiegman.

that celebration included John Oliver, now president of the Conservancy, and a relatively new superintendent for Ohiopyle State Park, Larry Adams. Although Adams was not on the train in 1975, he realized the potential of the long, nearly flat, right-of-way as an outstanding biking and hiking trail. He shared the vision of the original promoters.

As he began his tenure as superintendent of Ohiopyle State Park, Adams investigated ways to develop the trail. With the help of ingenious park maintenance staff, he built a spreader that could take crushed limestone and lay it evenly on the surface where the rails, ties, and most of the large heavy ballast had been removed. His connections with PennDOT helped him to obtain a used roller that could level and compact the limestone. Each year, Adams ordered crushed limestone for other park projects, but would add a little bit more than necessary "just in case he ran out." That extra was stockpiled out of the way behind the park office. Finally, with a spreader, roller, and enough crushed limestone to build about nine miles of trail, the experiment began. Starting at Ramcat Hollow on the south end of the park near Confluence, a trail slowly made its way toward Ohiopyle. In 1986, the first section of the Youghiogheny River Trail, later to become a part of the Great Allegheny Passage, quietly opened.

Visitors to the popular park quickly discovered the trail and rode with the same enthusiasm that filled the last WM train a decade before. People began to bring their bikes to the park and enjoy the ride along the middle Yough with its sweeping scenic vistas and short walks to the river's edge. That part of the river, which had previously been the province of kayaks, canoes, and rafts, could now be enjoyed from a terrestrial view. The first nine miles of bike trail was a huge success. So much so that visitors asked for more.

Soon the Youghiogheny River Trail was extended to the north and across the High Bridge, providing a grand view of Railroad Rapids upstream and the equally spectacular view downstream. Whooping and hollering rafters on com-

First section of the trail from Ohiopyle to Ramcat Hollow, Ohiopyle State Park, 1986. Photograph by Paul g Wiegman.

mercial trips floated seventy feet below cyclists as they enjoyed the smooth, fenced ride across the High Bridge. Later, the trail was completed to Bruner Run on one end and to near Confluence on the other. More visitors came and asked for even more trail.

People from surrounding areas soon took notice. In Somerset County, much of the Western Maryland right-of-way was still intact, but now in the hands of the CSX Corporation, which had consolidated the Chessie System and the Seaboard Coast Line in 1980. Joseph Kupec, a student at Indiana University of Pennsylvania, hiked the abandoned route in the summer of 1986. In a class report, he described his experience and suggested that since the land was still available, it could and should be made into a first-class biking and hiking trail, linked to the new trail in Ohiopyle State Park.

Hank Parke of the Somerset Chamber of Commerce read the report and arranged for Kupec to give a presentation to a handful of cyclists and conservationists in Somerset County. They responded positively and formed the Somerset County Rails to Trails Association. The purpose of the new organization was to investigate the possibility of acquiring the rest of the former Western Maryland Railway right-of-way and building the forty-two-mile Allegheny Highlands Trail from the Mason-Dixon Line to Confluence. There, the new trail would link with the Youghiogheny River Trail in Ohiopyle State Park.

After long negotiations and planning by local, county, state, and federal groups, the project began. Rockwood was selected as the place to begin, and in 1994 the first seven miles of the Allegheny Highlands Trail between Rockwood and Garrett opened to the public. At the celebration, Maynard Stembower watched the ribbon being cut.

Soon the popularity of the first miles of the Allegheny Highlands Trail stimulated more interest and more trail building in Somerset County. Constructing the first trail section between Rockwood and Garrett did not require dealing with any bridges or tunnels. Extension of the Allegheny Highlands Trail meant working with (or around) four major bridges over the Casselman River, two major viaducts, and two tunnels. Trail building went from an effort that could be handled by a crew of dedicated volunteers, local contractors, and tens of thousands of dollars to major rebuilding and the need for millions of dollars.

At the same time and closer to Pittsburgh, the popularity of the Youghiogheny River Trail in Ohiopyle State Park was also attracting

Spring along the Passage. Golden ragwort and flowering dogwood in bloom near Confluence.
Photograph by Paul g Wiegman.

261

attention. Cyclists were thinking of ways to access the trail without having to drive to Connellsville, Ohiopyle, or Rockwood. One novel idea was to run a weekend excursion train with a baggage car for bikes on the Pittsburgh and Lake Erie spur, which ran from the P&LE Station on Pittsburgh's South Side to Connellsville. In 1990, however, the P&LE abandoned the spur line to Connellsville. In response to the availability of this corridor, trail enthusiasts from Allegheny, Fayette, and Westmoreland counties created the nonprofit Regional Trail Corporation (RTC). The first action of the RTC was to buy the P&LE right-of-way and start building trails. By 1993, the initial portions of the Youghiogheny River Trail North were completed. New pieces were added each year through the 1990s, and the final connections between McKeesport and Connellsville were made in 2001. That same year, a trail was completed between Rockwood and the Pinkerton Horn in Somerset County. Together, all of these once isolated trails now connected for one hundred miles. Growing out of the segments of the Allegheny Highlands Trail, the Youghiogheny River Trail, and the Youghiogheny River Trail North, the Great Allegheny Passage was formed. Bike trail fever had spread across the Mason-Dixon Line into Maryland, where the Allegany County Highlands Trail of Maryland began in 1992, again following the path of the WM. By the fall of 2004, the first sections of the trail were opened from Frostburg to the Mason-Dixon Line.

In 1995, rail trail groups gathered at nearby Hidden Valley Resort to talk about their respective projects and share ideas. From that meeting, they formed the Allegheny Trail Alliance (ATA) to provide a single voice for the seven trails which were beginning to coalesce. The ATA, under the leadership of group president Linda Boxx, went beyond local funding to pursue state and federal funds. The DCNR had been fund-

ing the burgeoning trail since the first nine miles in Ohiopyle State Park. Under new federal transportation legislation, funds were available for nonautomotive transportation grants. The ATA and its various member groups used their collective impact to secure state and federal grants and raise considerable private foundation and individual member support. These funds enabled the huge task of resurfacing bridges, viaducts, and tunnels and making these structures, which were once an impediment to the original trail vision, usable as parts of the Great Allegheny Passage.

The biggest obstacle was the Big Savage Tunnel. Although only

3,294.6 feet long—only 0.4 percent of the whole 150-mile trail—it was absolutely necessary to integrate the Big Savage into the trail. The only ways around the tunnel through Big Savage Mountain were either up over a rocky path leading to the summit, or over a winding route from Deal, Pennsylvania, to Cumberland along steep and narrow roads. In early 2001, estimates for rehabilitation of the Big Savage Tunnel were just under eight million dollars. Both ends of the structure had collapsed after over twenty-five years of lack of maintenance in the harsh environment of some of the highest parts of Pennsylvania. Water filled the inner tunnel as ground seepage broke through the old railroad liner.

The contractor soon found new problems that would require more money than had been raised. The cycle of estimates exceeding available funds continued for months. Work sometimes came to a stop, and it occasionally appeared that the whole project might have to be abandoned.

Finally, with a total bill of over twelve million dollars, the Big Savage Tunnel was completed in 2003. The trail between Meyersdale, Pennsylvania, and the northwest portal of the tunnel was finished later that year. In back-to-back ceremonies in the spring of 2006, the trail groups and state and local governments dedicated both the Big Savage Tunnel and the final portion of the Great Allegheny Passage from the Salisbury Viaduct to the Mason-Dixon Line.

In December of the same year, the final nine miles of trail between Woodcock Hollow, Maryland, and Cumberland were dedicated in the shadow of the former Western Maryland Railway Station. With that final link opened, the vision of the Great Allegheny Passage from Cumberland to Connellsville was realized.

The dream was furthered when the Great Allegheny Passage was extended as far as McKeesport. During the time of feverish trail build-

ing along the Casselman and Youghiogheny rivers, trails were developed along Pittsburgh's three rivers—the Eliza Furnace Trail, the South Side Trail, and a trail leading from the former South Side steel works to West Homestead. Connection to McKeesport was a logical next step.

With the 250th anniversary of Pittsburgh in 2008, the completion of the Passage into the city became a prime objective. The rehabilitated Hot Metal Bridge, connecting the Eliza Furnace Trail and the South Side Trail, was dedicated in fall 2007. Work on the "gaps" in

the Great Allegheny Passage between McKeesport and Pittsburgh has been accelerated in order to complete as soon as possible the entire 150 miles of trail from Cumberland to Pittsburgh.

Just a small group of people rode that train in May 1975, but their enthusiasm was contagious. As more and more people shared the enthusiasm, volunteer trail builders, contributors, and finally trail users became part of a circle of people linked by a common love for the Great Allegheny Passage. That uncommon dedication to an uncommonly beautiful route highlighted by natural, industrial, and cultural history has produced a national treasure available to all those who take the time to enjoy and appreciate this uncommon passage.

Fall near Rockwood.

Salisbury Viaduct from Business Route 219 near Meyersdale.

Vista of the Ridge and Valley Province from just outside the southeast portal of the Big Savage Tunnel.

(right) Cyclists outside the northwest portal of the Big Savage Tunnel.

(left) Along the Great Allegheny Passage near Frostburg.

Western Maryland Scenic Railroad steam engine "Mountain Thunder" at the Western Maryland Railway Station, Cumberland.

Restored Western Maryland Railway Station at Cumberland, the southern end of the Great Allegheny Passage.

SOURCES

Abbot, W. W., Dorothy Twohig, Philander D. Chase, Beverly H. Runge, and Frederick Hall Schmidt, eds. *The Papers of George Washington, Colonial Series, 1748–August 1755*. Charlottesville: University of Virginia Press, 1983.

Anderson, Fred. *Crucible of War: The Seven Years' War and the Fate of Empire in British North America, 1754–1766*. New York: Alfred A. Knopf, 2000.

Anderson, N. "The General Chooses a Road." *Western Pennsylvania Historical Magazine*, September 1959.

Bailey, Kenneth P. *The Ohio Company of Virginia and the Westward Movement, 1748–1792: A Chapter in the History of the Colonial Frontier*. Glendale, CA: Arthur H. Clark Company, 1939.

Baldwin, Leland D. *The Keelboat Age on Western Waters*. Pittsburgh: University of Pittsburgh Press, 1941.

———. *Pittsburgh: The Story of a City, 1750–1865*. Pittsburgh: University of Pittsburgh Press, 1937.

Boucher, John N. *Old and New Westmoreland*. New York: The American Historical Society Inc., 1918.

Brumwell, Stephen. *Redcoats: The British Soldier at War in the Americas, 1755–1763*. Cambridge: Cambridge University Press, 2002.

Buck, Solon J., and Elizabeth Hawthorn Buck. *The Planting of Civilization in Western Pennsylvania*. Pittsburgh: University of Pittsburgh Press, 1939.

Buckley, Geoffrey L. *Extracting Appalachia: Images of the Consolidated Coal Company, 1910–1945*. Athens, OH: Ohio University Press, 2004.

Cupper, Dan. *Our Priceless Heritage: Pennsylvania's State Parks, 1893–1993*. Harrisburg: Pennsylvania Historical and Museum Commission, 1993.

Dederer, John Morgan. *War in America to 1775: Before Yankee Doodle*. New York: New York University Press, 1990.

Department of Community Affairs. *Heritage Parks; A Program Manual*. Harrisburg: Commonwealth of Pennsylvania, 1989.

Dickens, Charles. *American Notes.* 1850. New York: St. Martin's Press, 1985.

DiCiccio, Carmen. *Coal and Coke in Pennsylvania.* Harrisburg: Pennsylvania Historical and Museum Commission, 1996.

Ellis, F. *History of Fayette County, Pennsylvania.* Philadelphia, L. H. Everts, 1882.

Ewald, Johann. *Treatise on Partisan Warfare.* Translated, annotated, and with an introduction by Robert A. Selig and David Curtis Skaggs. New York: Greenwood Press, 1991.

Fitzpatrick, John C., ed. *The Diaries of George Washington 1748–1799.* Boston: Houghton Mifflin Company, 1925.

Ford, Jennifer L. "Landscape and Material Life in Southwestern Pennsylvania, 1798–1838." PhD diss., University of Pittsburgh, 2001.

Gallay, Alan. *Colonial Wars of North America, 1512–1763: An Encyclopedia.* New York: Garland Publishing, 1996.

Gipson, Lawrence Henry. *The British Empire Before the American Revolution, The Great War for the Empire: The Southern Plantations, 1748–1754.* New York: Alfred A. Knopf, 1967.

Gilpin, Joshua. "Journal of a Tour from Philadelphia thro the Western Counties of Pennsylvania." September 25, 1809, published serially in *Pennsylvania Magazine of History and Biography* 50–52 (1926–1928).

Hanna, Charles A. *The Wilderness Trail, or the Ventures and Adventures of the Pennsylvania Traders on the Allegheny Path.* New York: G. P. Putnam's Sons, 1911.

Harpster, John W., ed. *Crossroads: Descriptions of Western Pennsylvania, 1720–1829.* Pittsburgh: University of Pittsburgh Press, 1938.

Harvey, Katherine A. *Best Dressed Miners: Life and Labor in the Maryland Coal Region, 1835–1910.* Ithaca, NY: Cornell University Press, 1969.

Hinderaker, Eric. *Elusive Empires: Constructing Colonialism in the Ohio Valley: 1673–1800.* Cambridge: Cambridge University Press, 1997.

Hoffmann, Donald. *Frank Lloyd Wright's House at Kentuck Knob.* Pittsburgh: University of Pittsburgh Press, 2000.

Hofstra, Warren R. *The Planting of New Virginia: Settlement and Landscape in the Shenandoah Valley.* Baltimore: The Johns Hopkins University Press, 2004.

Ingham, John N. *Making Iron and Steel: Independent Mills in Pittsburgh, 1820–1920.* Columbus: Ohio State University Press, 1991.

Jackson, Donald, and Dorothy Twohig, eds. *The Diaries of George Washington, 1748–65.* Charlottesville: University Press of Virginia, 1976.

James, Alfred P. *The Ohio Company: Its Inner History.* Pittsburgh: University of Pittsburgh Press, 1959.

———, ed. *Writings of General John Forbes Relating to His Service in North America.* Menasha, WI: The Collegiate Press, 1938.

Jennings, Francis. *Empire of Fortune: Crowns, Colonies, and Tribes in the Seven Years' War in America*. New York: W. W. Norton and Company, 1988.

Kenny, James. "Journal of Col. John May, of Boston, Relative to a Journey to the Ohio Country, 1798." *Pennsylvania Magazine of History and Biography* 37 (1913).

Kent, Donald H. *The French Invasion of Western Pennsylvania*. Harrisburg: Pennsylvania Historical and Museum Commission, 1954.

Koegler, Karen. "Building in Stone in Southwestern Pennsylvania." PhD diss., University of Kentucky, 1992.

Koegler, Karen, and Kenneth Pavelchak. "From Cumberland to Wheeling, West Virginia." In *A Guide to the National Road*, edited by Karl Raitz. Baltimore: Johns Hopkins University Press, 1996.

Kopperman, Paul E. *Braddock at the Monongahela*. Pittsburgh: University of Pittsburgh Press, 1997.

Lorant, Stefan. *Pittsburgh; The Story of an American City*, 5th edition. Pittsburgh: Esselmont Books, 1999.

Lubove, Roy. *Twentieth Century Pittsburgh*. Vol. 2, *The Post-Steel Era*. Pittsburgh: University of Pittsburgh Press, 1996.

Madarasz, Anne. *Glass: Shattering Notions*. Pittsburgh: Historical Society of Western Pennsylvania, 1998.

McCardell, Lee. *Ill-Starred General: Braddock of the Coldstream Guards*. Pittsburgh: University of Pittsburgh Press, 1958.

McConnell, Michael N. *A Country Between: The Upper Ohio Valley and Its Peoples, 1724–1774*. Lincoln: University of Nebraska Press, 1992.

McGuinness, Marci, and Bill Sohonage, *The Explorer's Guide to the Youghiogheny River Gorge/Ohiopyle and South West Pennsylvania's Villages*. Ohiopyle, PA: Backwoods Books, 2000.

McMurry, Sally. *From Sugar Camps to Star Barns*. University Park, PA: The Pennsylvania State University, 2001.

Louis Mulkearn, ed. *George Mercer Papers Relating to the Ohio Company of Virginia*. Pittsburgh: University of Pittsburgh Press, 1954.

Netting, M. Graham. *50 Years of the Western Pennsylvania Conservancy: The Early Years*. Pittsburgh: Western Pennsylvania Conservancy, 1982.

Palmer, Tim. *Youghiogheny: Appalachian River*. Pittsburgh: University of Pittsburgh Press, 1984.

Pargellis, Stanley, ed. *Military Affairs in North America, 1748–1763: Selected Documents from the Cumberland Papers in Windsor Castle*. Hamden, CT: Archon Books, 1969.

Peyser, Joseph L. *Jacques Legardeur de Saint-Pierre: Officer, Gentleman, Entrepreneur*. East Lansing: Michigan State Press, 1996.

Phillips, Don. "Whatever Became of the Western Maryland Railroad, Part I, Going Out as It Came In—Quietly." *Trains*, May 1980.

Reese, George, ed. *The Official Papers of Francis Fauquier, Lieutenant Governor of Virginia, 1758–1768*. Charlottesville: University Press of Virginia, 1980.

Reiser, Catherine Elizabeth. *Pittsburgh's Commercial Development. 1800–1850*. Harrisburg: Pennsylvania Historical and Museum Commission, 1951.

Report of the Pittsburgh Flood Commission. Pittsburgh: Flood Commission of Pittsburgh, 1912.

Shank, William H. *The Amazing Pennsylvania Canals*. York, PA: American Canal and Transportation Center, 1981.

———. *Great Floods of Pennsylvania*. York, PA: American Canal and Transportation Center, 1972.

Stevens, Sylvester K., Donald H. Kent, Autumn L. Leonard, eds. *The Papers of Henry Bouquet, December 11, 1755–May 31, 1758*. Harrisburg: Pennsylvania Historical and Museum Commission, 1972.

Smith, Roland M. "The Politics of Pittsburgh Flood Control, 1908–1936." *Pennsylvania History* 42 (1975).

Southwestern Pennsylvania Heritage Commission and National Park Service. *America's Industrial Heritage Project Action Plan*. Washington DC: U.S. Department of Interior, 1989.

Stegmaier, Harry I., Jr. et. al. *Alleghany County: A History*. Parsons, WV: McClain Printing Co., 1976.

Trego, Charles. *A Geography of Pennsylvania*. Philadelphia: Edward C. Biddle, 1843.

Toker, Franklin. *Fallingwater Rising: Frank Lloyd Wright, E. J. Kaufmann, and America's Most Extraordinary House*. New York: Alfred A. Knopf, 2003.

Valentine, Alan. *The British Establishment 1760–1784: An Eighteenth Century Biographical Dictionary*. Norman: University of Oklahoma Press, 1970.

Wall, Joseph Frazier. *Andrew Carnegie*. New York: Oxford University Press, 1970.

Ward, Matthew C. *Breaking the Backcountry: The Seven Years' War in Virginia and Pennsylvania, 1754–1765*. Pittsburgh: University of Pittsburgh Press, 2003.

Warren, Kenneth. *Triumphant Capitalism: Henry Clay Frick and the Industrial Transformation of America*. Pittsburgh: University of Pittsburgh Press, 1996.

Washington, George. *The Journal of George Washington: An Account of His First Official Mission, Made as Emissary from the Governor of Virginia to the Commandant of the French Forces on the Ohio, October 1753–January 1754*. Williamsburg, VA: Colonial Williamsburg, 1959.

West, Martin, ed. *War for Empire in Western Pennsylvania*. Ligonier, PA : Fort Ligonier Association, 1993.

Wood, Joseph S. "The Idea of a National Road." In *The National Road*, edited by Karl Raitz. Baltimore: The Johns Hopkins University Press, 1996.

CONTRIBUTORS

JENNIFER FORD is a consulting historian specializing in the development of interpretive plans and exhibits for museums and historic sites. She has worked with a wide variety of sites, including Old Economy Village, the Pennsylvania Lumber Museum, the Stevens & Smith Historic Sites, Somerset Historic Center, and the Senator John Heinz History Center. A theatrical lighting designer for many years, she also breeds show-quality alpacas and owns Backstage Alpaca, a boutique in Bedford, Pennsylvania, which sells designer alpaca clothing and textiles.

ROBERT GANGEWERE is the retired editor of *Carnegie Magazine,* a founding member of the Friends of the Riverfront, and a board member of the Allegheny Trail Alliance. He has produced many heritage signs along regional trails. His publications include *The Bridges of Pennsylvania and Allegheny County* (2001). He is currently writing a history of the Carnegie Museums of Pittsburgh.

EDWARD K. MULLER is professor of history and director of the Urban Studies Program at the University of Pittsburgh. He is coauthor of *Before Renaissance: Planning in Pittsburgh, 1889–1943* (2006), editor of

DeVoto's West: History, Conservation, and the Public Good (2005), and co-editor of *North America: The Historical Geography of a Changing Continent* (2001). He is former chair of the board of directors for the Rivers of Steel National Heritage Area and former member of the board of trustees of the Senator John Heinz History Center.

KEVIN J. PATRICK is professor of geography and regional planning at Indiana University of Pennsylvania. He is coeditor of *Pittsburgh and the Appalachian: Culture and Natural Resources in a Postindustrial Age* (2006), author of *Pennsylvania Caves and Other Rocky Roadside Wonders* (2004), and coauthor of *Diners of Pennsylvania* (1999).

MARTIN WEST is director of Fort Ligonier. He received the Pennsylvania National Guard Meritorious Service Medal for history advocacy. He served on the Mt. Vernon Advisory Council of George Washington Scholars, annotated Washington's autobiography in *George Washington Remembers* (2004), and was a University of Pittsburgh adjunct lecturer.

PAUL G WIEGMAN is a freelance naturalist/writer/photographer. He writes a column for the *Pittsburgh Tribune Review* and the *Pittsburgh Quarterly* magazine. He is a former naturalist-at-large and later vice president for science and stewardship for the Western Pennsylvania Conservancy. With the Conservancy he worked on the team initiating the first efforts to build a biking/hiking trail on the Western Maryland Railway right-of-way. He is compiling a comprehensive history of the development of the Great Allegheny Passage and working on other projects about western Pennsylvania. He is on the board of the Somerset Rails to Trails Association and is treasurer of the Allegheny Trail Alliance.

INDEX

Great Crossing, 80, 99, 218–19
Great Depression, 192, 211
Greater Pittsburgh Parks Association, 212. *See also* Western Pennsylvania Conservancy
Great Gorge Trail, 61
Great Lakes, access to interior via, 157
Great Meadows, 80, 85, 92
Greene County, 123–24, 176
green salamander, 30

H. C. Frick Coal and Coke Company, 179–80
H. C. Frick Coke Company, 12
Hagan, I. N., 213
Hagerstown, MD, 174
Hannastown, PA, 119–22
Harnedsville, PA, 252, 255
Harris, Thaddeus, 130
Haystack Mountain, 24, 28, 52
Hazelwood, PA, 183–84
Heinz, Henry John, 184, 216
Hintz, Robert, 256
historic preservation, 206, 225; of Carrie Furnaces, 227–28; of coal heritage, 230–31; of C&O Canal, 234–35; environmental movement and, 231; Rivers of Steel National Heritage Area, 226–28; of Seven Years' War sites, 236
homes: for industrial workers, 188–89, *189*; John Frew's, *139*; log cabins, 133–37, *135*; log houses, 134, 137–38, *138*; non-log, 138–39
Homestead Strike, 156, 190–91, *193*
Homestead Works, 180, 182, 227, *229*
Hot Metal Bridge, *51*, 183–84, 228, 265, *266*
Houstoun, Mrs., 126–27, 147
hunting, by Native Americans, 76
hunting and fishing camps, 7–8, 210–11

Illinois Country (*pas des Illinois*), *77*
Illinois Territory, 127
immigrants: British, 187; European, 187; German, 124, 142–43, 187; Irish, 187; Scots-Irish, 124; as western settlers, 122–23; working in industries, 186–87, 192
Indian Creek, conservation program for, 230
industrial capitalism, Pittsburgh as example of, 189
industrialization, 10, 147, 184; along transportation routes, 5, 157; of glassmaking, 163–64; steam power in, 169; water power in, 208
industry, 6, 159; factories closing, 7, 192, 224–27; preservation of heritage, 226–28. *See also* specific industries
Interstate 68, 204
iron making, 164, 184; coke making and, 175–76, 178; conditions in, 188–89; Pittsburgh's dom-

inance in, 5, 181, 183; preservation of heritage of, 227; railroads and, 173; in western Maryland, 5, 186
iron ore, 5. *See also* natural resources
Iroquois Confederacy, 76–78

Jacob's Creek, silica for glassmaking in, 161
Jennings Creek, 36
Joe Magarac myth, 187–88, *188*
Jonathan Run, 48, 208
Joncaire, Philippe Thomas Chabert de, 82
Jones and Laughlin (J&L): American Iron Works, 180; Hot Metal Bridge connecting plants of, 183–84; mill sites on trail, 183; mines and coke works of, 13, 178; Soho Works, *185*
Jumonville, Joseph Coulon de Villiers de, 85–86, 88–89
Jumonville Glen, 86, 201–2

Kaufmann, Edgar J. and family: at Bear Run, 211, 213
Kennywood amusement park, 228
Kentuck Knob, 213
Keystone Viaduct, 232, *242*, 253, 255
"Klondike" area, Lower Connellsville District as, 177
Kreigbaum, MD, 36
Kruger, Karl, 219
Kupec, Joseph, 259–60

labor: conditions in mines and mills, 188–89; preservation of heritage of, 230–31
labor relations: disputes in, 189–92; Homestead Strike, 156
land: Pennsylvania and Virginia's conflict over, 4; sales of, 116–17, 122–23; settlers clearing, 133–34; speculation, 79, 116, 156, 160, 179; Western Pennsylvania Conservancy and, 212–13, 248
La Salle, René-Robert Cavelier de, 78
Latrobe, PA, 177
Laurel Highlands, 13, 202, 236
Laurel Highlands Hiking Trail, 248
Laurel Hill, 80
Laurel Hill Creek, 43–44, 230
Laurel Ridge: forests in gorge of, 53–56; rock pleats of, 28; Youghiogheny River through, 26, 28, 205
Laurel Ridge State Park, 212–13
Laurel Ridge Water Gap, 31
Laurel Run, 36
Leilich, George M., 249
Lick Run, 38, 60
Ligonier, John Louis, 106
limestone, 24, *195*

Washington County, 123–24, 176

Washington DC: accessing interior via, 158, 208; C&O Canal Towpath going to, 2; railroad service to, 7; relations with hinterlands, 10, 11, 13, 143

Waterford, PA, 82

The Waterfront, on Homestead Works site, 227

water gaps, 21, 26, 48

Water Obstructions Act of 1913, 255

Wayne, Anthony, 122

Western Maryland Project. *See* Great Allegheny Passage trail

Western Maryland (WM) Railway, 6, 173–74; abandoning tracks, 2, 7; bought by B&O, 234–35; bridges of, *196, 222, 254, 257*; in Chessie System, 224, 245; compared to B&O, 224; creative engineering by, 232; demise of, 246–47; easy grade of, 247; first train on, 253; last train on, *246*; management's pride in, 247, 256; officially abandoning railroad, 248–49; promotional ride by, 245–46, 249–53, *250–52*, 266; removal of tracks, 224; route of, 36, 205, 223–24; stations of, *225, 243*, 264, *274*; trails following route of, 228, 232; trees growing up in right-of-way, 55–56; wanting to give land for bike trail, 223, 247–48, 256

Western Maryland Scenic Railroad, *199*, 232–33, *273*

Western Pennsylvania Conservancy: acquiring land, 212–13, 256–57; in creation of Great Allegheny Passage trail, 2, 248, 254–58; increasing interest in conservation and, 7–8; Kaufmann's donations to, 213; state parks and, 212–14, 248; Western Maryland's promotional ride and, 246, 249–53

West Homestead, PA, 184

Westinghouse, George, 184

Westmoreland County, 176; in border dispute with Virginia, 119–20; creation of, 118–19; early mill in, *145*; German influence in, 124, 143; Path of Progress through, 231

West Newton, PA: navigation to, 167, 172; railroads to, 172–73; Whiskey Rebels in, 160

West Overton, PA, 161

West Virginia Central Railroad, 174

Wheeler Flats, bridge over, *71*

Wheeling, West Virginia: B&O Railroad to, 171; National Road Heritage Corridor to, 236; National Road to, 126, 158

Whetzel, Joshua, Jr., 248, 255–56

whiskey, 129, 159; farmers' stills, 142–43; Overholt distillery, 12, 160–61; tax on, 11, 160

Whiskey Rebellion (1794), 11, 160

Whites Creek, 207

whitewater rafting, *109*, 259; at Ohiopyle, 202–3,

219–23, *221*; over Pottsville series, 31; popularity of, 7, 256; on the Youghiogheny rapids, 46–47

wildflowers, along Great Allegheny Passage trail, 60–67

wildlife, along Great Allegheny Passage trail, 29–30, 59

Wills Creek, 28, 82; B&O following, 36, 223–24; Nemacolin's Path from, 79–80, 90, 92; Ohio Company trading post on, 79

Wills Creek Valley, age of rocks in, 25

Wills Mountain, 24, 52; Nemacolin's Path going over, 79–80; water gap carved through, 28, 233

wind turbines, 38, *244*

Woodcock Hollow, MD, 264

Wright, Frank Lloyd, 213

Wyandot people, the, 88

Youghiogheny Dam, 44, 214, 218–19

Youghiogheny Loop, 210, 221

Youghiogheny Navigation Company, 167–68

Youghiogheny River: appearance of, 44, 48; as barrier to National Road, 207; boating on, *31*, 220–23; bridges over, *196, 251–52*, 255; changing directions, 45; confined by bulkheads in Connellsville, 48; at Confluence, *197, 198*; confluence with Casselman River, 42–44, *43*; confluence with Monongahela, 33, 48, 216, 228; erosion by, 26–28, 205; flood-control lake above Confluence on, 7; glassworks along, 163; gradient of, 45; Meadow Run joining, 203; navigation on, 5, 166–68, 172; Nemacolin's Path meeting, 80; obstacles to navigation on, 132, 203; at Ohiopyle Falls, 45; Pottsville sandstone in, 30; railroads following, 224; rapids on, 46, *46*, 109–10; in relation to Great Allegheny Passage trail, 45–48; river conservation program for, 230; seeds transported by, 63; settlements along, 123, 145–46; settlers moving west on, 127–28; whitewater rafting on, 219–23, *221*

Youghiogheny River Trail, 232; connected into Great Allegheny Passage trail, 232, 259–60, 262; first stretch opened, 258–59, *259*; popularity of, 260–62

Youghiogheny River Trail North, 3, 228, 262

Youghiogheny River Trail South, 3

Youghiogheny River Water Gap, 22, *58*

Youghiogheny Valley: forests in gorge of, 53–56; as microclimate, 63–64; railroads in, 6, 208, 224; uses for, 205–6

Youngstown, Ohio, 173